# The Tragedy of Heterosexuality

# The TRAGEDY of HETEROSEXUALITY

Jane Ward

NEW YORK UNIVERSITY PRESS

*New York*

**NEW YORK UNIVERSITY PRESS**
New York
www.nyupress.org

First published in paperback in 2022

Library of Congress Cataloging-in-Publication Data
Names: Ward, Elizabeth Jane, author.
Title: The tragedy of heterosexuality / Jane Ward.
Description: New York : New York University Press, [2020] | Series: Sexual cultures |
Includes bibliographical references and index.
Identifiers: LCCN 2020004725 (print) | LCCN 2020004726 (ebook) |
ISBN 9781479851553 (cloth ; alk. paper) | ISBN 9781479804467 (pb)
ISBN 9781479895069 (ebook) | ISBN 9781479892792 (ebook)
Subjects: LCSH: Heterosexuality. | Sexual minorities. | Feminist theory.
Classification: LCC HQ72.8 .W37 2020 (print) | LCC HQ72.8 (ebook) | DDC 306.76—dc23
LC record available at https://lccn.loc.gov/2020004725
LC ebook record available at https://lccn.loc.gov/2020004726

*For straight women.*
*May you find a way to have*
*your sexual needs met*
*without suffering so much.*

# Contents

# 1

# LET'S CALL IT WHAT IT IS

## The Tragedy of Heterosexuality

I AM WORRIED ABOUT STRAIGHT PEOPLE. AND I AM NOT
the only one. Queer people have been concerned about straight culture
for decades, not only for our own sake—because we fear homophobic
violence or erasure of queer subculture—but also because straight culture's impact on straight women often elicits our confusion and distress.
Erotically uninspired or coercive, given shape by the most predictable
and punishing gender roles, emotionally scripted by decades of inane
media and self-help projects, and outright illogical as a set of intimate
relations anchored in a complaint-ridden swirl of desire and misogyny,
straight culture for many queers is perplexing at best and repulsive at
worst. And yet queer people often leave the issue alone because no matter how worrisome straight culture may appear to us, we know all too
well the problems with denying people their erotic attachments or critiquing an entire population's sexual orientation.

Am I am being hyperbolic when I say I am worried about straight
people? Granted, this is an unfamiliar way of thinking about heterosexuality for most straight, and many gay, people. Living under the weight of
heteronormativity means that a lot of people have come to understand
heterosexuality as the most instinctive and fulfilling form of sexual relating. We are subject, as children and adults, to an onslaught of institutions and media images that link basic human happiness and nearly all
significant rites of passage to heterosexual desire and coupling. And,
as many queer people will attest, it can be very difficult—depressing,
shameful, lonely, frightening, vulnerable, violent, and traumatic—to be
lesbian, gay, or bisexual. Many queers have wished to be straight, and

many have come to the conclusion that the undeniable easiness of heterosexuality relative to queerness is evidence of the idea that no one "chooses" to be queer—what rational person would choose a life of antigay oppression? Through the lens of queer suffering, it seems almost ludicrous to feel concern for straight people, at least not on account of their straightness. For straight people experiencing other violent and dehumanizing forms of oppression—poverty, white supremacy, patriarchy, ableism, religious discrimination—straightness offers a degree of respectability and privilege. As the African American feminist and activist Barbara Smith explained in 1979, "Heterosexual privilege is usually the only privilege that Black women have. . . . Maintaining 'straightness' is our last resort."[1] Straightness is a means through which people can access some (unearned) cultural and institutional rewards vis-à-vis the marginalization of their queer counterparts. Straightness ameliorates other forms of suffering and creates an easier life. So if being straight makes life easier, why on earth would queer people spend any time feeling worry or sympathy about the effects of straight culture on straight people's lives and relationships?

This book argues that the basic premise of this question—that heterosexuality is easier than queerness—requires renewed investigation. For instance, if we were to take this premise to the contemporary lesbian feminist Sara Ahmed, we would be encouraged to consider that one of the ways heteronormativity sustains itself is by telling and retelling a story about how heterosexuality makes people happy, while queerness produces difficulty and suffering. This story about queer suffering under the force of heteronormativity is true; but it is also only a sliver of the story about queerness, and it is one that masks not only queer joy and pleasure but also queer relief not to be straight. The story about the benefits of heterosexuality is also one with wildly differing levels of truthfulness, or explanatory power, once subjected to an intersectional analysis. The late lesbian feminist poet and theorist Adrienne Rich contended that while being straight was largely beneficial for men, the same was not always true for women, for whom the institution of heterosexuality had been a site of violence, control, diminishment, and disappointment. Similarly, straight Black feminists, from Michelle Wallace to Brittney Cooper, have long raised questions about the gap between the promises of heteronormativity and the realities of Black women's relationships with men. Straight Black men benefit considerably from straight relationships, while, as Cooper explains, "the privileges of straightness [have] eluded me and a whole generation of overachieving Black women."[2] Perhaps most urgently, an important indicator of the relatively negligible value of heterosexuality for many women is the fact that their sexual relationships with men have been maintained by force, both through cultural propaganda targeting girls and women and more directly through sexual assault, incest, compulsory marriage, economic dependence, control of children, and domestic violence. This book will provide ample evidence of these dynamics. The question, then, is, Is heterosexuality optimal for women when it requires so much coercion?

Gay men, especially white gay men, are often the greatest defenders of the narrative about queer suffering, probably because they have more power and privilege to lose as a result of inhabiting a nonnormative sexual orientation (and sometimes a nonnormative gender). Relatedly, gay men are also more likely than lesbians to embrace biological theories of sexual orientation and the corresponding claim that people are only gay because they have no choice in the matter. These perspectives have drowned out lesbian feminist discussions about erotic agency and the appeal of queer joy, and they have prevented us from investigating the various ways that a woman might respond when, to use Cooper's phrase, the privileges of straightness elude her. It is my belief that gay men's persistent ownership of the meaning and origins of queerness, along with many gay men's lack of concern about the lives of women, has made it difficult to shift our attention away from what is sad about being gay to what is even sadder about being straight. My aim is to show that when we hold the relationship between misogyny and heterosexuality in full view, we are able to see beyond the male-centric claim that queerness constitutes a tragic and unwilled loss of power, a loss that no one would ever choose (even as it brings sexual pleasure and fosters the "pride" of the oppressed). Still today, misogyny is rarely ever meaningfully scrutinized in mainstream gay-rights discourse, so the reasonable suggestion that women stand to gain more than they lose by extracting themselves from heterosexual culture and cultivating queerness has become nearly impossible to hear amid the born-this-way chorus. For all of these reasons, I am of the mind that lesbian feminist critiques of heterosexuality, now sometimes dismissed as outdated, have renewed relevance and urgency.

This book is about a critical but still largely overlooked consequence of the drowning out of lesbian feminist ideas and experiences. When lesbian feminist ideas are sidelined, we keep our focus on queer misery, and we fail to name the contradictions and miseries of *straight culture*— the entrapment, the disappointment, the antagonism, the boredom, the unwanted sex, the toxic masculinity, and the countless daily injustices endured by straight women. This book is about the failure to recognize these not only as feminist problems but more specifically as *straight problems* that many queer women are wildly grateful to have escaped. While conservatives have long promoted the belief that queer relationships are unnatural, damaged, and fraught with various kinds of dysfunction, this project examines what might be gained from raising similar questions about the health and sustainability of heterosexual culture—a culture arguably damaged by misogyny, even as it has been unwilling to address the structural causes of this damage.

I will show that the narrative about the "tragedy of queerness"—the seemingly gender-neutral claim that no one would ever wish queerness upon themselves—does not reflect many queer women's lived experiences. And yet there is no denying that countless lesbians have adopted this narrative. Is it possible that this story about the tragedy of queerness is more a rhetorical habit, an idea we've internalized from gay men— not to mention worried family members, bad television, or the church? Some years ago, I was chatting about parenting with a lesbian couple with a child close in age to my own. We arrived at the topic of children's sexuality, and one of the lesbian moms made a comment I have heard before, a comment that lesbian and gay people are perhaps more likely to share openly than lefty straight parents: "If I am to be totally honest, I would prefer, for our child's sake, that he isn't gay. We don't want him to have to deal with the challenges that come with being gay." Despite the stark reality of homophobic bullying, this logic didn't ring true to me, and I was struck by how normalized it had become to say something about queerness ("No one would choose to be gay" or "I don't want my child to be gay like me") that most people I know would be quite unlikely to say about almost any other form of difference subject to violence and oppression. I then asked these lesbian moms, "Do you *really* feel that way? Do you feel like your own life has been so terrible that you wish your parents could have saved you from it? Do you feel that being straight would have been better for you?" These women both smiled, looked at each other, laughed, and said, "No. I see your point." I didn't probe further, but what I imagined those sly smiles were reflecting was their instantaneous flashback to all that was pleasurable and joyous about their lesbian lives. I have no idea what they were actually thinking, but the point here is that I suspect many queers love (the queer part of) their lives, even when they have been trained to rehearse a narrative about how hard and tragic it all is. This narrative bolsters heteronormativity not only by obscuring the profound forms of queer joy that accompany and often compensate for queer suffering but also by implying that heterosexual lives are free of gendered violence and suffering.

Let me be clear. Homophobic violence happens—to young people and adults, to women, men, and trans people. It happens to straight people when they are gender variant and/or are presumed to be queer. And it happens most harshly to queer people of color and poor and working-class queers. In all cases, it is tragic. The ideas behind the popular 2010 "It Gets Better" campaign—namely, that queer kids can expect to grow up, become autonomous, make money, and discover their entitlement and civil rights—were critiqued, for good reason, for eliding the persistent race, class, and gender disparities that shape the lives of many queer people.[3]

But misogynistic and racist violence happens to straight people too, and in many ways, gendered and sexualized and racist forms of violence and suffering are much more unrelenting for straight women than for anyone else. When I teach "Introduction to Gender and Sexuality Studies" at UC Riverside, I show a series of documentary films about gendered violence and suffering. These are films about the horrific violence (sexual, physical, emotional) that women endure at the hands of men and the state, about the incredible toll that masculinity takes on men's bodies and mental health (as well as women's bodies and mental health), and about the tedium and unequal division of labor that destroys, or threatens to destroy, an astounding number of heterosexual relationships. Even though I have seen these films a dozen times, I still cry when I watch them, and I have always assumed that I am crying feminist tears. I have assumed I am crying for women. But more recently, something shifted. After watching the films, rereading the numerous articles about gender oppression I had assigned, and listening to countless stories from straight women students about their abusive or just plain not-feminist male partners, I got in my car and breathed a huge sigh of relief that I am queer. I went home and told my partner, "Thank god we are queer." And I realized that I was crying queer tears for straight people. It became clear to me: Straight women's lives are very, very hard. It's not that it "gets better" for queer people; it's that heterosexuality is often worse.

Often anger is the dominant mode of relating to heterosexuality among radical queers. But this book argues that it is more appropriate to *worry* about heterosexuals, to feel empathy, to "call them in" rather than call them out, and ideally, to be in solidarity with them as they work to liberate heterosexuality from misogyny. Here I take inspiration, in part, from the queer worry expressed by the dazzling figure of Aunt Ida (played by Edith Massey) in John Waters's 1974 cult film *Female Trouble*. In an unforgettable scene in which Aunt Ida counsels her straight-identified nephew Gator that she'd be so happy if he "turned nelly," she begs of him, "But you could change! Queers are just better. I'd be so proud of you as a fag. . . . I'd never have to worry. [But now], I worry that you'll work in an office, have children, celebrate wedding anniversaries! The world of heterosexuals is a sick and boring life." Like Aunt Ida, I reverse the direction of the "ally relationship," such that queers become concerned allies to the straights in our families and communities, especially the women who may be experiencing more gendered suffering than we are, and without the hot sex, queer humor, and political solidarity to which many of us queers have access.

There is no doubt that my own queerness, femmeness, whiteness, able-bodiedness, and position as a scholar living in the United States have shaped, and limited, my ways of thinking about straightness. To understand the intersectional complexities of lesbian feminist critiques of straightness, I have leaned heavily on the writings of queer feminists of color and placed their insights at the forefront of my analysis. I could not be more grateful to have access to their pathbreaking work, much of which offers an extraordinary model of how to balance critique and love, pain and solidarity. To the straight people reading this book, let me say with all my love and solidarity, I am your ally.

## The Tragedy of Heterosexuality: A Lesbian Feminist Diagnosis

Let me quickly assure you that this book is not so much about straight people themselves but about the straight culture in which they are embedded and to which they are held accountable. As with the often nebulous racial category of whiteness, one of the ways that we avoid looking critically at straightness is to keep it indefinable, to imagine that it is so vast and irreducible to any one way of being. A queer person makes a critical statement about straightness to which a straight person will object: "How can you say that? There are so many different kinds of straight people. Many straight men, like my husband/boyfriend/brother, are gentle and feminist. Many straight relationships are egalitarian, loving, and based on feminist principles." We might even characterize these claims as #notallstraightpeople. And of course these claims are true.

They also function, however, to invalidate queer critiques of straight culture, to silence or otherwise shut down queer witness testimony about the straight world. As when white people protest that critiques of racism should not tar all whites with one brush, the intention behind this kind of request to avoid "overgeneralizations" is typically to focus on exceptions. Many people like to identify with the exceptions, which soften the sting of critique and accountability. So let us acknowledge those exceptions. Feminist straight men, and feminist men's projects, *do* exist (though I can count the ones I know personally on one hand, maybe two). Men do more housework and parenting labor than they used to (though not much more, recent evidence suggests).[4] Some straight people live queer-ish lives, engaging in polyamory, heteroflexibility, kink, marriage refusal, and so forth, though it is unclear the extent to which these practices challenge the real problems at the heart of straight culture. There are straight couples that are very happy. There are men who love and respect women deeply. There are men who were raised by feminists, lesbians, and lesbian feminists. There are men who are attracted to aging women, hairy women, fat women, powerful women, and feminist women. But none of these feminist modes of relating have made much of a dent in *straight culture*, the subject of my analysis.

So what is "straight culture," as seen through a queer, feminist lens? As this book will explore in depth, queer/lesbian complaints about straight culture have circulated around two overarching themes (with several additional subthemes considered in the chapters to follow).[5] First, queer feminists have argued that straight life is characterized by the inescapable influence of sexism and toxic masculinity, both of which are either praised or passively tolerated in straight spaces. Second, queer observers of straight life have pointed to straight women's endless and ineffective efforts to repair straight men and the pain of witnessing straight women's optimism and disappointment. While some queers might now balk at the idea of spending our precious time theorizing heterosexuality or standing in solidarity with straight women, these were central projects for lesbian feminists in the 1970s and '80s.[6] Lesbian feminists thoroughly documented and theorized the tragedy of heterosexuality beginning in the early 1970s, though they used different terms and came to different conclusions than my own. Their archive is vast, and I offer only a very quick a summary here.

As for the normalized sexism inside straight culture, lesbian feminists wrote volumes. With righteous rage, they detailed the ways that straight men desired women's services—emotional, sexual, reproductive, domestic—rather than actual women, and they exposed the toll this took on women's mental health. The Radicalesbians declared, "by virtue of being brought up in a male society, we have internalized the male culture's definition of ourselves . . . as relative beings who exist not for ourselves, but for the servicing, maintenance, and comfort of men."[7] They described recoiling from men's misogyny ("I began to avoid him, . . . to sleep with him to shut him up, to be silent out of exhaustion, to take tranquilizers . . .").[8] Audre Lorde described sex with men as "dismal and frightening and a little demeaning."[9] Gloria Anzaldúa recounted the misogyny inside straight Mexican culture, wherein "woman is the stranger, the other, . . . man's recognized nightmarish pieces, his Shadow-Beast. The sight of her sends him into a frenzy of fear," and consequently, Anzaldúa explains, "I made the choice to be queer."[10] Kate Millet put forward a theory of patriarchy as a heterosexual political system maintained through men's sexual power over women, in families as well as in the public sphere, that had naturalized rape and other forms of men's sexual coercion and control of women.[11] Cherríe Moraga concurred that the "control of women begins through the institution of heterosexuality," adding that a man wants "to be able to determine how, when, and with whom his women—mother, wife, and daughter—are sexual. For without male-imposed social and legal control of our reproductive function . . . Chicanas might freely 'choose' otherwise, including being sexually independent from and/or with men."[12]

Lesbian feminists noted that even men on the left, the seemingly good men who promised to respect women, ultimately caused women tremendous suffering. Andrea Dworkin, who is now often vilified for her

fervent opposition to porn, BDSM, and sex work, came to lesbian feminism after experiencing severe physical and sexual abuse at the hands of
her anarchist activist husband (he hit, kicked, burned, and raped her)
and subsequently engaging in sex work for survival. Dworkin experienced multiple other instances of misogynistic violence in her life, and
as she delved more deeply into feminist work, the astounding ubiquity
and normalization of misogyny and men's violence against women became clear to her: "I heard about rape after rape, . . . women who had
been raped in homes, in cars, on beaches, in alleys, in classrooms, by
one man, by two men, by five men, by eight men, hit, drugged, knifed,
torn, women who had been sleeping, women who were with their children . . ."[13] In the mid-1970s, at the height of lesbian feminist writing,
marital rape was legal in every state in the United States, and hence, rape
was understood by lesbian feminists not only as an act of patriarchy but
also as a normalized expression of heterosexuality. Though not a lesbian
but arguably queer, the African American feminist scholar bell hooks,
too, described the frequency with which straight women fled abusive
relationships with ostensibly enlightened men: "Individual heterosexual women came to the movement from relationships where men were
cruel, unkind, violent, unfaithful. Many of these men were radical thinkers who participated in movements for social justice, speaking out on
behalf of the workers, the poor, speaking out on behalf of racial justice.
However when it came to the issue of gender they were as sexist as their
conservative cohorts."[14] As lesbian feminists witnessed radical straight
men remain in denial about patriarchy, many gave up on the feminist
possibilities for straight men and for straight relationships.

During the 1970s and '80s, lesbian feminists also established that while
sexism was a foundational element of straight culture, how sexism mani-
fested itself in women's lives was significantly variable (what would later
be termed "intersectional"). Race, culture, socioeconomic class, and re-
ligion produced specific forms of heteropatriarchy, and hence, straight
culture itself was never monolithic. In 1977, the Black feminist members
of the Combahee River Collective Statement, many of whom were queer,

theorized that the forces of white supremacy and heteropatriarchy often overlapped, serving two functions at once ("[Black girls are] told in the same breath to be quiet both for the sake of being 'ladylike' *and* to make us less objectionable in the eyes of white people").[15] Like white lesbian feminists, Black and Chicana lesbians detailed men's violence against women partners and family members, but they also extended this analysis to radical movements (the Black Nationalist movement, the Chicano power movement), contexts in which women of color were expected to provide service to men and to follow men's leadership.[16] Though not a lesbian feminist text, Michelle Wallace's 1978 feminist classic *Black Macho and the Myth of the Super Woman* painted a powerful image of the self-sacrifice expected of straight Black women vis-à-vis the racist oppression of Black men: "Every time she starts to wonder about her own misery, to think about reconstructing her own life, to shake off her devotion and feeling of responsibility, to everyone but herself, the ghosts pounce. . . . The ghosts talk to her. *You* crippled the Black man. *You* worked against him. *You* betrayed him. *You* laughed at him. *You* scorned him. *You* and the white man."[17] Wallace, echoing the Combahee River Collective, knew that antiracist political solidarity with men was vital to the survival of women of color but that true liberation must also center an analysis of patriarchy. In similarly intersectional work, Chicana lesbian feminists, including Cherríe Moraga, Gloria Anzaldúa, and Carla Trujillo, showed that one-dimensional concerns about the effects of racism on men of color (and not women) were exacerbated by religious and cultural beliefs about women as natural caretakers; both sets of beliefs intersected to amplify women's sense of emotional, sexual, and political duty to men.[18] Similarly, lesbian feminist analyses of socioeconomic class, such as found in the essays of the white, working-class lesbian writer Dorothy Allison, illuminated the ways that white, working-class cultural values—self-sacrifice, silence, survival, and tradition—reinforced men's control over women inside straight relationships.[19]

Lesbian feminists were also alarmed by the amount of time and energy straight women were investing in trying to gain men's respect, with either painfully slow or nonexistent results. In 1972, the women's caucus of the Gay Revolution Party issued a statement in which they expressed serious concern that straight women "seem to believe that through their attempts to create 'new men' they will liberate themselves. Enormous amounts of female energy are expended in this process, with little effect; sexism remains the overwhelming problem in the most 'liberated,' 'loving' heterosexual situations."[20] The white lesbian separatist Jill Johnston pronounced that she was identifying as a "woman committed woman" rather than a "feminist," explaining, "so many feminists advocate a change in our situation in relation to the man rather than devotion of our energies to our own kind."[21] Lesbian feminist writers also documented the ways that girls and women were groomed by straight culture to desire relationships with men despite the overwhelming evidence that heterosexual relationships were unequal. The promise of love and happiness, according to Adrienne Rich, was the lure that seduced girls and women into a thinly veiled relationship of subjection. As Rich explains, "the ideology of heterosexual romance, beamed at her childhood out of fairy tales, television, films, advertising, popular songs, wedding pageantry, is a tool ready to the procurer's hand and one which he does not hesitate to use."[22] Lesbian feminist writing made exceedingly clear the contradictions and precariousness of heterosexuality as a system equally organized around love and abuse, manifest in the story told to countless little girls: "He hit you because he likes you." Indeed, as feminist historians have argued, this exchange of potential love and protection for servitude is, historically speaking, heterosexual romance's defining moment.[23]

## A Mountain of Evidence

But let us get more specific and more current. Part of why it is important to return to classic lesbian feminist texts, and why lesbian feminist ideas have arguably been making a comeback of late, is because so much has not changed or has been repeatedly subject to men's antifeminist backlash. As I write, every major media outlet has attempted to make sense of the ubiquity of straight men's sexual harassment and sexual assaults of women (what the media is calling "the wake of #metoo"). Multiple states are enacting abortion bans with the aim of overturning *Roe v. Wade* at the federal level. Currently, the president of the United States and many men in Congress are shamelessly displaying their misogyny with regularity and great entitlement. This is all happening on the political stage, and it's also happening in girls' and women's daily lives, in their relationships with boys and men.

It is difficult even to know where to begin the project of cataloguing the daily violence that men commit against girls and women in the name of love and desire. We could start with childhood, wherein adult men who work as writers for Disney/Pixar are still using the big screen to communicate to little girls that finding a prince makes magic happen, changes the world, wins wars, beautifies everything, and brings girls closer to the divine.[24] We could look to high schools, where sex education teachers are still training girls in how to relate to themselves as (inevitably straight) sexual victims and gatekeepers and to boys as sexual agents and predators.[25] We could take notice of the fact that blatant expressions of misogyny have become the commonplace language of heterosexual sex itself ("fuck that bitch," "murder that pussy," "beat that pussy up," "grab her by the pussy," "choke her out," "dig her out," "nail her," "pound her," and so forth).[26] We would also want to examine the ways that so many boys and men value other men's approval more than women's humanity, continuing a now centuries-old tradition of positioning bros before hoes and using control over women's bodies to earn male respect,[27] to make money for men,[28] and to reroute their disavowed desire for one another through a more socially acceptable object.[29] We might choose to focus, as the Chinese feminist journalist Leta Hong Fincher has done, on the role of the state in encouraging women to embrace men's mediocrity, to pretend to desire men they do not want, and to roll back their own accomplishments for the good of the nation.[30] We could look closely at recent findings that the hopeful story about the new, engaged father has been greatly exaggerated and that straight women across race, class, and job status still do the majority of the child-care work.[31] We could steel ourselves for the sociologist Gloria González-López's brave and chilling study of father-daughter and uncle-niece incest in Mexico, in which she demonstrates that the script of heterosexual romance has helped to normalize incest by cultivating men's attraction to girls and young women in need of care or rescue, by cultivating women's attraction to men of higher status than themselves, and by recirculating the idea that men have unstoppable sexual needs that women are obligated to meet.[32] We could also consider the gravity of the sociologist Diana Scully's argument, based on interviews with seventy-nine convicted rapists in the United States, that rape happens as frequently as it does because so few boys and men have been trained to identify with girls and women, to empathize with their experience, and to humanize them.[33]

The tragedy of heterosexuality is about all of this and more. There are complex and multiple forms of heterosexual suffering that vary according to women's positions within hierarchies of race, socioeconomic class, and immigration status. To understand this suffering, we could also look, as the Black feminist criminologist Beth Richie does, at the ways Black women in the criminal justice system have been seduced and entrapped by the expectation that they will be made happy by, and must remain loyal to, Black men—even as some of these men rape, beat, and torture them and their children.[34] We could turn to research by indigenous feminists that shows, in brutal detail, the way that settler-colonial violence has shaped indigenous heterosexuality and its miseries (through the imposition of white colonial gender norms; through the theft of land, resources, and culture that sustained community health and cohesion).[35] We could examine—as numerous feminist writers have—the white-supremacist structures that sustain white boys' and men's profound sense of entitlement to women's bodies and attention and their willingness to yell at, stalk, threaten, rape, shoot, and kill women who dare to be unavailable or uninterested.[36] We could notice, as demonstrated by the South Asian American feminist scholar Shamita Das Dasgupta, that immigrant women often hide their husbands' violence because they are under pressure to present an "unblemished" image of their families and communities in order to avoid racist discrimination and state terror.[37]

We might also examine the patriarchal and white-supremacist anchors of heterosexual desire in the United States, where Asian American women and white men are consistently ranked "most desirable" in surveys, with the former valued for beauty and docility and the latter for power.[38] We might decide to place a spotlight on the sad state of heterosexual sex itself—the coercion,[39] the missing female orgasms,[40] girls' and women's agreement to sex so as "to get it over with" or "be nice." And we could, and should, keep a watchful eye on the copious ways that straight culture repackages itself to make all of these tragic injustices appear inevitable, if not desirable: bioevolutionary theories about the needs of cavemen, the tsunami-like force of testosterone, and the unavoidable nature of locker-room talk;[41] biblical justifications for strong male leadership and the return to a more harmonious prefeminist era;[42] self-help books designed to help straight women rediscover their lost femininity and turn over the reins to men (explored in chapter 2); and the persistent maligning of feminist and queer strategies and interventions that stand to address the root causes of these problems.[43]

When my last book was published,[44] I heard from many gay male critics that they disagreed with my argument that straightness can be understood as a fetish for normalcy, and queerness as a desire for the unexpected and counternormative. Several gay men wrote to me and explained that this argument made no sense to them since "every gay man wants to be normal" or has wished that he were straight.[45] These men, though speaking from their experience as gay men, seemed to have generalized their aspirations for normalcy to queer people more broadly. They seemed to believe that wishing for the ease and privileges of heterosexuality is part of every queer person's lot in life. But as I hope my brief review of the tragedy of straight culture has illuminated, this argument simply does not hold water when we pay even a modest amount of attention to heterosexuality as a *patriarchal institution*, one that has long benefited men and harmed women.

Furthermore, while the daily tedium of heterosexual culture, characterized in part by a predictable and incessant wellspring of antagonisms and unresolved complaints (often termed "the battle of the sexes" by mainstream commentators), is less violent than many of the aforementioned examples, it is nonetheless distressing. One of the sadder features of straight culture, as the lesbian feminists quoted earlier made clear, is that straight people keep going back for more, even as men don't seem to like or respect women much at all and as feminist straight women (at least in my experience) are quick to confess that they have little respect for men. Often propelled by the essentialist and heteronormative logic that male and female "energies" are incomplete without each other or that "opposites attract" or that heterosexual desire is hardwired and nonnegotiable, straight culture seems to rely on a blind acceptance that women and men do not need to hold the other gender in high esteem as much as they need to *need* each other and to learn how to compromise and suppress their disappointment in the service of this need.

## Are Straight Women Okay?

These compromises take strange and varied forms that can easily produce shock and concern for feminist queers. In my now forty-five years as an observer of the straight world, I have noted that it appears to be perfectly acceptable for straight couples to share few interests, to belittle or infantilize each other, or to willingly segregate themselves during important moments in their relationships. Straight couples experience significant rites of passage like weddings and baby showers nearly separate from each other, even though these rituals, at least theoretically, are intended to signify something about the evolution of their partnerships. Many straight women spend dozens of hours planning each detail of their weddings or baby showers or baby gender-reveal parties, while straight men keep their distance from the very rituals that are intended to mark important moments in their lives. In no way do I intend to imply that couples should spend every minute together, but if we held straight couples to basic standards of good friendship—mutual respect and affection and a sense of comfort and bondedness based on shared experience—many straight relationships would fail the test. This is precisely the observation that led Erin Sullivan, a blogger for the popular lesbian website *Autostraddle*, to write the essay "Are Straight Women Okay?"[46] Though lighthearted in tone, Sullivan's review of products marketed to straight couples—husband and wife "conversation starter" cards, his and her coffee mugs in which the "his" mug is larger than its counterpart, and a novelty "sex check book" that helps straight couples maintain a fair sexual balance of giving and receiving—compels her to ask, "Are straight woman okay? Like, not in a joking way—do they need assistance?" In a follow-up essay, she extends her alliance to straight women, pondering how to best reach them: "I'm not sure where we go from here. Do we put up flyers? Wear a special pin? Maybe when you see [straight women] at a Pride event this month crowding the very bar you're trying get a drink from, make sure to remind them that we are their allies in this fight and then wait for instruction."[47]

Concern about straight women's well-being, and agreement that straight men would benefit considerably from some basic instruction on how to treat women, is something of a running joke in queer subculture—or, to be more accurate, in dyke subculture. For instance, the Instagram page @hets_explain_yourselves is a digital archive of #hetnonsense that includes in its bio the rhetorical question "Are Hets OK?" Followers of the page can scroll with befuddlement or horror through images of infant clothing proclaiming, "I heart boobs just like daddy," a beer garden called "Husband Day Care Center," numerous memes about how to keep a man, a diet book that promises women they can use nutrition to control the gender of their future babies, and so on. In a similar vein, the queer comedian DeAnne Smith has a comedy routine based on precisely this blend of queer shock and confusion about straight people's lives. Speaking first to straight women and later to straight men, Smith proclaims during her routine,

> I don't know how to speak to straight women but I do have something to tell you. . . . You have set the bar in your relationships *too low*. How would *I* know that? . . . The girl I am dating now, until now, has exclusively dated men. It is *so* easy to impress her! . . . It is ridiculous. I just show her basic human decency and she loses her mind. . . . Straight guys, it's not that hard to impress women. Show minimal, minimal, minimal, *minimal* interest in things your lady is passionate about. . . . Take care of your ladies. I don't have time for all of them.

Perhaps something like white audiences' laughter at the work of Black comedians whose humor hold ups a mirror to centuries of white violence and inhumanity, straight audiences laugh at Smith's disarming suggestion that basic human decency is missing from straight men's relationships with women. The joke is "funny" in part because pointing to many straight men's egomania and unbridled sense of entitlement is simultaneously shocking (anyone who dares to seriously make this claim is met immediately with the #notallmen brigade or worse), but it is also familiar. It's funny because it's true.[48]

In addition to wondering about whether most straight men and women have a foundation of mutual interest or respect, another question that queers sometimes ponder about straight people is whether they are actually sexually attracted to one another. Studies show that many straight-identified women find penises "unattractive," are "turned off" by images of nude men, and prefer to gaze at naked women when given the option.[49] We also know that girls and women consent to a tremendous amount of sex with men that they don't want to have and/or that is not pleasurable and that straight women are frequently in relationships with men for reasons other than attraction (financial security, obligation, to retain resources for children, etc.). For instance, in an essay titled "What I Would Have Said to You Last Night Had You Not Cum and

Then Fallen Asleep," the feminist blogger Reina Gattuso illuminates the banality of straight women's dissatisfying sexual experiences with men as she reflects on her orgasmless recent sexual experience with a "decent guy." Speaking as if directly to this decent but self-centered male sex partner, the representative of "anyman, everyman," she explains,

> You're a decent guy. . . . I do not feel like you are going to rape me. . . . The sex wasn't particularly bad, either. . . . It was normal sex. Normal, boring, vaguely dehumanizing hetero sex. Which is precisely the point: The normalcy. . . . Because there was something in the choreography of the whole thing that just struck me as, I don't know—unsatisfying in a way only feminism can remedy. . . . Here, supposedly, is what you consider sex: We make out, you play with my boobs, I blow you, you do not go down on me even though I ask [*insert some bullshit on how "I only go down on women I'm in love with. Now put it in your mouth."]. Penis goes in vagina, penis moves in and out of vagina, . . . penis ejaculates. . . . Sex is now over because you have decided it is over. You have decided sex is over because you are a man, and because this choreography that favors men with penises—man becomes erect, man penetrates woman, man ejaculates—is what we have been told sex is.[50]

While straight men's desire for women's bodies is often portrayed as an incredibly powerful force, many men's notorious confusion about what produces female orgasm, their disinterest in providing oral sex to women, and their dramatically narrow ideas about what constitutes a female body worth desiring (waxed, shaved, scented, dieted, young, etc.) suggests that heteromasculinity is characterized by a much weaker and far more conditional desire for women's bodies than is often claimed. To lesbians, men's countless missed opportunities to actually like women are baffling.

Even what passes as heterosexual intimacy is often resented by straight women who find themselves doing the emotional heavy lifting for men who have no close friends and won't go to therapy. Men are less likely than women to discuss mental health with friends and family, to seek out psychotherapy, or to recognize they are depressed—a pattern so common as to be termed "normative male alexithymia" by psychologists.[51] For straight men in relationships, all of these needs get aimed at women partners. In 2016, the writer Erin Rodgers coined the term "emotional gold digger" to describe straight men's reliance on women partners to "play best friend, lover, career advisor, stylist, social secretary, emotional cheerleader, mom."[52] Elaborating on this dynamic and the emotional burnout it produces in straight women, Melanie Hamlett further explains that the concept of the emotional gold digger "has gained more traction recently as women, feeling increasingly burdened by unpaid emotional labor, have wised up to the toll of toxic masculinity, which keeps men isolated and incapable of leaning on each other. . . . While [women] read countless self-help books, listen to podcasts, seek out career advisors, turn to female friends for advice and support, or spend a small fortune on therapists to deal with old wounds and current problems, the men in their lives simply rely on them."[53] Similarly, in the book *Eloquent Rage*, the feminist Brittney Cooper points to men's striking absence as supportive figures in her life, a role that is filled by other straight women friends. Cooper explains, "When my patriarchal nuclear fantasy didn't happen and the privileges of straightness eluded me and a whole generation of overachieving Black women, it is my girls who have celebrated my success, showered me with compliments, taken me out on dates, traveled the world with me, supported me through big life decisions, and showed up when disasters struck." As other straight feminists have concluded before her, Cooper wonders if "perhaps straight women need to become less invested in the project of straightness altogether. . . . Far too many women leave behind the freedom feminism offers because they want to stay on patriarchy's dick, which is to say they want to secure their straightness and their options of getting chosen."[54]

All of this evidence that women get a raw deal in relationships with men does not suggest, however, that straight women are not "really straight" and should just go ahead and become lesbians, or celibate, already. While many lesbian feminists actually made this argument in the

1970s, my analysis of the tragedy of heterosexuality has brought me to a very different conclusion. While I view Cooper's suggestion that women should "become less invested in straightness" as an important option, later I will argue that another way forward is to redefine heterosexuality itself, to expand its basic ingredients to include more, and not less, attachment and identification between women and men.

While a detailed analysis of the origins of sexual orientation is beyond the scope of this book, which is concerned with straight *culture*, it is important to note that sexual desires are developed by a complex of forces that are not always conscious to us, or under our control. For instance, from a Freudian perspective, human infants have an expansive capacity to experience pleasurable sensations in response to humans of all kinds, one's own bodily functions, and even objects and animals that are soft or interesting to the touch. This expansive desire gets disciplined to conform to social norms, with heterosexual desire being the primary imperative communicated to most children. As I have summarized elsewhere, the cultural theorist Sara Ahmed offers a powerful account of the way heterosexual desire is reproduced, passed on by parents, as both an obligation and a "gift," to their children: "[For Ahmed] . . . the child's entire social world is oriented toward heterosexuality while other object orientations are cleared away. Heterosexuality, as the intimately close, familiar, normalized, and celebrated couple formation, is the space in which the child lives and becomes the space in which the child feels 'at home.' The child's body itself, like bodies desiring familiar foods, gets shaped by its cultural context and begins to tend toward the familiar."[55] Queerness, too, is shaped in part by forces beyond our control, but I am not a believer that these forces are hormonal or neurological. It is quite possible, for example, that children who are attuned to the tragedy of heterosexuality, or who are keen observers of the misery wrought by heteropatriarchy in the lives of their parents or other significant adults, are oriented otherwise by a desire to avoid such suffering. This may well have been my own story, no matter how much my queerness now feels animated by the raw hotness of butch dykes and other queer objects of my lust.

## Where Patriarchy and Heteronormativity Intersect

Some readers might wonder whether the problems that this book describes are best understood under the umbrella of patriarchy, rather than heterosexuality. Why focus on straightness at all? There is no doubt that the problems that plague straight culture are the problems of patriarchy, or men holding power over women, and this means that the tragedy of heterosexuality requires feminist intervention. But patriarchy is also too blunt a conceptual instrument to capture the nuances of heterosexual dysfunction, in part because, as the gender theorist Judith Butler has argued, the relationship between patriarchy and heterosexuality is more mutually constitutive than unidirectional.[56] Heterosexuality (or the investment in a normative sexuality organized around the attraction of opposite bodies) is not an outgrowth of preexisting binary gender differences but a force that requires and *produces* binary gender difference. In other words, the tragedy of heterosexuality is about men's control of women, but it is also about straight women's and men's shared romantic and erotic attachments to *an unequal gender binary*, or to the heteroerotic fantasy of binary, biologically determined, and naturally hierarchical gender oppositeness. This last feature, straight culture's eroticization of men's power over women, is often presented as a kind of benign playfulness—a joke shared among straight women about how husbands always get away without doing their fair share, let's say. But the heteroerotic appetite for situations in which straight men can display power over women also fuels sexual violence, infusing straight culture with endless eroticized representations of men hurting women and with romantic tales of the redemption of violent, aggressive, entitled, and self-obsessed straight men.

This is not to say that we shouldn't eroticize gender differences. Gender differences are hot! Queer subculture delights in celebrating what is sexy about a whole array of ever-evolving gender expressions (nonbinary genders, gender fluidity, femme, butch, and the broad spectrum of gender expressions that go by the name trans); but queer people also increasingly agree that these gender expressions are not determined by people's body parts or sex assignment at birth, nor are they linked to sexual desire in any predictable way (femmes are often attracted to femmes, queers of all stripes can find nonbinary folks desirable, and so forth). There is no doubt about it, straight culture's obsession with genital-based gender and sexual identity (i.e., only women can be feminine and only people with vaginas can be women) is one of its defining features, one that influences how straight people understand not only what is sexy but also what is safe and equitable. Straight culture encourages panic at the idea that someone of "the wrong sex" might be using the women's restroom and thereby threatening women's sexual safety, while a queer approach to safety broadens our analysis to include gender policing and gendered violence of *all* kinds—including violence against trans and nonbinary queers who just need to pee and face no end of harassment in public bathrooms. Similarly, straight culture's version of gender equity often looks like men taking on "women's work" (housecleaning, child care) but needing a *ton* of gender affirmation in the process or using their strength and privilege to lovingly protect the girls and women in their lives.[57] These changes make a certain kind of progress, but they rely on and sustain well-worn, binary notions about the roles of men and women that make many queer people cringe.

Typically, when there is a general consensus that something is terribly disappointing or dysfunctional, like a new restaurant or a workplace policy, let's say, that disappointing thing is shut down, protested against, revised in some form—unless that thing is heterosexuality, for which there is an uncanny attachment to returning, after no end of complaint or disappointment, right back to its original form. Adrienne Rich addressed this problem by highlighting that while numerous feminist writers have made it their life's work to document the expansive list of ways that heterosexuality fails women, these same writers have all too often authorized this failure by being unable to imagine an alternative or by treating heterosexuality as an inevitable biological inclination that "does not need to be explained." Rich goes on to say that despite lesbianism being an arguably more logical and fulfilling arrangement for women, it is "lesbian sexuality which . . . is seen as requiring explanation."[58]

Pop feminist texts, such as Hanna Rosin's buzz-worthy 2012 book *The End of Men: And the Rise of Women*, are notorious for producing heterofeminist complaints that ultimately go nowhere except back to blaming women for being too dominant and successful or for setting their romantic standards too high.[59] Queer critiques of Rosin's book point not only to the failures of this kind of pop-feminist project and its conclusions but more generally to the tragedy of heterosexuality, itself "the sinking ship." Of Rosin's book, the queer scholar Jack Halberstam explains, "Like a romantic comedy that throws up every objection to the coupling of the male and female leads only to manufacture some farcical event that brings them back together again and makes them see the error of their ways, Rosin shows men and women moving in radically different directions and then concludes that maybe we need to opt again for traditional gender roles to right the sinking ship of marriage, family, and the social world built on the bedrock of heterosexuality."[60] For straight women like Rosin, who are intimately bound to men, the need to tend to male feelings and preserve male entitlements is the cost of making a degree of feminist progress (i.e., as Rosin details, women are now equitably represented in the workforce and in universities and are performing well in those spheres, for instance). The feminist writer Leta Hong Fincher documents a similar bind for upwardly mobile Chinese women in her book *Leftover Women: The Resurgence of Gender Inequality in China*. The professional and university-educated young women whom Fincher interviewed described their boyfriends as selfish, jealous, insensitive, boring, arrogant, and generally unappealing, and yet they also described a high likelihood that they would marry these men because they did not believe better men were available and they feared being lonely.[61] This tragic arrangement on which heterosexuality was founded—"I don't really like you, but I am going to get (or stay) married to you out of fear or practicality"—remains alive and well, giving rise to an enormously profitable self-help and relationship-coaching industry designed to smooth over heterosexual antagonisms and disappointments.

My aim in the following chapters is to describe the tragedy of heterosexuality in sufficient detail that we might be able to make some sustainable queer feminist interventions into straight suffering, while also laying to rest once and for all the idea that queer women have any reason to envy straight culture or to mourn its loss in our lives. In fact, queer women have a long history of attempting to forge places away from the influence of straight culture (communal households, lesbian land, etc.), not simply to get away from straight cisgender men but to take respite from witnessing the tragedy of heterosexuality more generally.

My partner and I take this respite every summer when we visit a genderqueer feminist friend who lives in Hawaii, a woman we initially heard about through mutual friends but had never met. She used to live happily among a sea of queers in Berkeley, California, but after needing to move to a remote part of Hawaii for family and health reasons, she found herself without much of a queer community. So she put out a call through the queer feminist grapevine for queers to come visit. She missed queer people so much that she opened her home to us (and others) without having ever met us. Now she is family to us, and we bring new queers with us when we go. But it is also a no-straights-allowed kind of arrangement, which makes some of our straight friends look at us askance. And yet I understand perfectly that our friend has plenty of straight people in her social circle already; and even though many of these straight people are kind and good and feminist, the point is that queer people yearn for one another, and they yearn for a break from witnessing straight life.

All of this said, my intention is not to romanticize queer life. Being queer hardly means we are saved from sexual abuse, intimate-partner violence, unhealthy relationships, or traumatic breakups. Queer people act out and hurt each other in numerous ways, including violence, addiction, lying, and so forth. But the key difference between straight culture and queer culture in this regard is that the latter does not attribute these destructive behaviors to a romantic story about a natural and in-escapable gender binary. Lesbians, for instance, do not find ourselves attracted to a gender category that is principally defined by its inability to understand or identify with our own. We are not mansplained by the people who claim to love us. We are not expected by our partners to shoulder the most devalued household and parenting labor because we are women. On the whole, misogyny has not cast a shadow of fear over our flirtations. Our relationships, unlike straight relationships, aren't presumed to be subject to gender-based antagonisms or in structural conflict from the start. We are not always already set up in such a way that someone risks being a nagging wife or feeling trapped or need-ing to buy self-help best sellers like *He's Just Not That into You* or *Men Who Hate Women and the Women Who Love Them* or *How to Date Men When You Hate Men* or worrying about how to catch a man and keep him or resenting that our gender means we will do most of the parenting and housework or needing to convince our dating pool that we aren't bitches, whores, stupid, weak, or available to be grabbed by the pussy.

Quantitative data on quality-of-life comparisons between straight and queer women are not easy to come by, and within this limited body of research, one study often conflicts with another. There is evidence that lesbians have significantly more orgasms than straight women do,[62] engage in a more equal distribution of household labor than hetero-sexual couples do,[63] have higher earnings than straight women do,[64] have better-adjusted children than heterosexual couples do,[65] and, in some countries, report higher relationship happiness than heterosexual women do.[66] Other studies suggest that lesbians get divorced at rates equivalent to heterosexual women, though the meaning of this finding is unclear given that same-sex marriage is a recent phenomenon.[67] Some studies report similar rates of intimate-partner violence among lesbian couples and heterosexual couples, but questions remain about whether lesbians are more likely to report violence than heterosexual women are and/or are more likely to have their relationships misperceived by po-lice.[68] I approach all of this data with caution, as so much of the quantitative research on LGBT life tends to be motivated by a conservative or neoliberal agenda (e.g., antigay research finds that queer people are miserable and die young; progay research finds that queers are normal citizens, happily monogamous, and excellent parents).[69] Suffice it to say that the kind of quantitative data that would be most useful to the queer feminist investigation at hand are, by their very nature, limited. The field of critical heterosexuality studies is still in its infancy, and "straight culture," so hegemonic as to be unnamable outside of queer space, is a relatively new object of inquiry.

## The Paradox

One of the core dysfunctions of straight culture—and a centerpiece of my analysis—is the *misogyny paradox,* wherein boys' and men's desire for girls and women is expressed within a broader culture that encourages them to also hate girls and women. If you have experienced life as a girl or woman, you know the misogyny paradox all too well. Men shout "compliments" about girls' and women's bodies on public streets ("You are looking mighty fine today!" or "You're a beautiful woman. Why don't you smile?") and then, a moment later, when they are not met with a response, hurl violent and misogynistic threats ("Fuck you bitch!").[70] Young boys cannot wait to have sex with girls, and once they do, many describe girls' bodies in the most abject terms possible, seemingly disgusted by their very objects of desire.[71] Men love women's bodies, we are told, but only after women spend an inordinate amount of time whipping their bodies into a lovable shape—by dieting, shaving, waxing, dying, perfuming, covering with makeup, douching, and starving them. Young men, we are encouraged to believe, have a lot of desire for women, but they dare not talk to each other about sex in ways that center girls' and women's pleasure, power, or subjectivity because, paradoxically, this kind of talk feels *gay.* Such was the paradox that Jason Schultz, a feminist writer, was faced with when he wanted to have a nonsexist bachelor party and suggested to his male friends that they actually talk about sex and desire together ("What makes us feel sexy?") rather than hire a stripper.[72] When my students read about Schultz's alternative bachelor party, they are struck by how "gay" it seems, even as Schultz's request was for straight men to share stories, sans sexism, about their experiences of having pleasurable sex with women.

Sometimes, the misogyny paradox takes a dramatic and violent form, such as when men rape and/or murder women they purport to have desired or even loved. For instance, by twenty-two-year-old Elliot Rodger's own account, he shot and killed six college students in Isla Vista, California, in 2014 because he desired the girls he saw on campus but could not bear that his desire wasn't returned (as he said in his suicide video, "I don't know why you girls aren't attracted to me, but I will punish you all for it"). Violent expressions of the misogyny paradox appear frequently in popular culture, taking the form of men's "animal attraction" to women they simultaneously desire and loathe for talking too much, saying no to sex, being vain or disloyal, and so on. According to the documentary filmmaker Sut Jhally, this theme—men want women and also hate women—appears across musical genres and reproduces itself anew in each generation.[73] Perhaps no one has been a more brazen and high-profile exemplar of the misogyny paradox than President Donald Trump himself, a man who has bragged publicly that "no one loves women more" than he does and also bragged about sexually assaulting women. In mundane everyday life, however, the misogyny paradox takes the subtler form of straight men claiming to love women and yet speaking over them, explaining things to them with no regard for women's knowledge or expertise, and training their sons to reproduce this lack of respect for women's humanity. As explored in the chapters to follow, what is paradoxical here is not only that straight men say they love women and then turn around and express their misogyny but also that this love/hate relationship is successfully marketed to straight people as a source of happiness despite overwhelming evidence that it is a primary contributor to straight people's misery. As we will see, many straight women find themselves dating or married to men who feel to them like tyrants or children, and many straight men find themselves with women they don't actually want to talk to; both parties learn to fake interest in the name of relationship success.

In some ways, this paradox bears resemblance to the one examined by the sociologist Arlie Russell Hochschild in her 2016 book *Strangers in Their Own Land: Anger and Mourning on the American Right*. Hochschild traveled to rural Louisiana—where waterways are among the most polluted in the nation—to ask how it is that poor southern whites whose land, water, and bodies have been devastated by industrial toxicity continue to vote for probusiness conservatives committed to deregulation and, hence, environmental destruction.[74] In other words, why do poor southern whites undermine their own best interests? Hochschild finds the answer in a complex mix of rural whites' gratitude for their industrial jobs, their Christian belief that God will ultimately restore any human damage done to the Earth and to their own bodies, and their belief that the government cannot be trusted to help them. Similarly, in attempting to understand the misogyny paradox, we might ask how it is that so many women are investing in straight relationships, when these relationships so often cause them damage? The queer theorist Lauren Berlant's analysis of "cruel optimism"—the term she uses to describe "the condition of maintaining an attachment to a significantly problematic object"—may be useful here. Berlant asks, "Why do people stay attached to conventional good-life fantasies . . . when the evidence of their instability [and] fragility . . . abound?" People persist in these attachments, Berlant explains, because the fantasy object provides a "sense of what it means to keep on living and looking forward to being in the world."[75]

Cruel optimism strikes me as an apt lens through which to think about straight people's attachments to heteropatriarchy. The promises of heteropatriarchy are central to most ideas about what it means to live a good life: children are tracked toward heterosexual romance in their earliest years; boys and men achieve legible/successful masculinity largely through sexual access to women and their labor; and girls and women achieve value—and "happiness"—through access to male desire and approval. But when confronted with insurmountable evidence that heteropatriarchal arrangements are not all they have been promised to be, then what? It is this moment of disillusionment, or the discovery of the cruelty of the heteroromantic fantasy, which sets the stage for this book.

## What's Ahead

I hope to have sufficiently introduced the idea of the tragedy of heterosexuality and pointed to the work of several other queer/lesbian writers who have attempted to document, theorize, and dismantle it. Next I will move back in time, tracing the emergence of companionate marriage as a difficult but worthwhile heterosexual ideal, as well as the evolution of self-help texts and "relationship science" offered to straight couples to help them understand why women and men do not naturally like each other and how they might learn to cultivate, or at least present the appearance of, mutual affection. We begin with an examination of eugenicist "marital hygiene" texts of the early twentieth century, move on to a survey of midcentury advertising campaigns and educational films, and conclude with the late-century explosion of a self-help industry built on biopsychological claims about gender difference.

I will lay the historical groundwork for understanding how both misogyny, in the form of husbands' violent aversion to their wives, and white supremacy, in the form of eugenicist campaigns for white marital harmony, shaped American heterosexuality through the twentieth century and into the current period. The lens is focused on the particular ways that white Americans labored to produce heterosexual empathy and mutuality and Black Americans labored to produce heterosexual recognition and respectability, from the moment the term "heterosexuality" was invented and imported from Europe.

Narrowing our view of the heterosexual-repair industry, chapter 3 describes my ethnographic study of the international industry of "pickup artists" and "seduction coaches" for straight men. Here we will take a queer tour through an evolving industry that provides straight men around the globe with access to expert coaches—usually, but not always, men—who will teach them "the game," or how to seduce women. While straight women constitute the overwhelming majority of consumers of relationship self-help books, the seduction industry—with its tactical, scripted, and scientific approach to attracting the opposite sex—has been extraordinarily popular with straight men since 2005. Drawing on field notes from two weekend-long seduction bootcamps, interviews with seduction coaches, weekly updates and newsletters about how to seduce women, and over one hundred videos and webinar clips from pickup-artist bootcamps and in-field trainings around the globe, we will take a dyke's-eye view into the industry's sympathetic embrace of the "average frustrated chump," or the schlub who never gets the hot girl. Seduction coaches do the tripartite work of helping straight men grieve their imagined birthright (access to sex with hot women), normalizing men's sexual failures by explaining the evolutionary and sociocultural causes of sexual rejection using what they call "dating science," and teaching men to perform new styles of self-made masculinity aimed at making straight women feel safe, seen, and humanized.

I hope to reveal that this development of a "woke" masculinity, a masculinity that empathizes with straight women and recognizes their need to protect themselves against the hordes of manipulative and aggressive men, is a troubling and complex maneuver, one that reflects the proliferation of instrumental feminisms aimed at men's self-protection (legal liability), profit (the co-optation and commodification of social justice messages), good public relations, and in this case, sex. I show that for seduction coaches, "seeing the world through women's eyes" is a pragmatic strategy designed to bridge the gap between men's desire for sex with young, hot women and women's desire for humanization.

Next we take a step back from the heterosexual-repair industry, examining the misogyny paradox through a different lens: the lens of queer people's sympathies and frustrations with straights. Drawing on queer subcultural materials and interviews with queer people about straight culture, here I make the case that it is time to spill the tea—to reveal what queer people say about straight people behind closed doors so that we may help save straight people from themselves. Taking love and empathy as core elements of my methodology, here I explore the profound potential of reversing the "ally relationship" such that queer people offer feminist intervention and queer guidance to straight people suffering under the weight of the misogyny paradox.

I conclude the book with a meditation on the possibilities and promises of deep heterosexuality. Drawing on the diagnoses of heterosexual culture offered by the queer commons in chapter 4, here we honor the basic impulse of heterosexuality—that is, opposite-sex love and attraction—but imagine how this impulse might be taken to its most humane and fulfilling, and least violent and disappointing, conclusion. Calling on the wisdom of the dyke experience—wherein lust, objectification, humanization, and friendship live in complementary relationship to one another—here we remind straight men about the human capacity to desire, to fuck, and to show respect at the same time.

It is possible for straight men to like women so much, so deeply, that they actually really *like* women. Straight men could be so unstoppably heterosexual that they crave hearing women's voices, thirst for women's leadership, ache to know women's full humanity, and thrill at women's freedom. This is how lesbian feminists lust for women. I do not despair about the tragedy of heterosexuality, because another way is possible.

# 2

# HE'S JUST NOT THAT INTO YOU

## The Misogyny Paradox

Ｏｎ ａ ｒｅｃｅｎｔ ｖａｃａｔｉｏｎ ｗｉｔｈ ｍｙ ｐａｒｔｎｅｒ, ｋａｔ, ａｎｄ ｏｕｒ nine-year-old son, we strolled by the storefront of a touristy T-shirt shop. There were hundreds of T-shirts for sale inside the store, but a few, presumably some of the shop's most popular, were displayed in the front window. One of the T-shirts hanging in the window depicted an image of a stick-figure straight couple on their wedding day; she is smiling, and he is frowning. The text below them reads, "Game Over." A T-shirt just next to this one showed another stick-figure straight couple holding hands while the woman figure's mouth is open, with speech lines indicating that she is talking. Next to this image, the same couple is depicted again, except the male figure has hit or pushed the woman, and she is falling down, head first. The text below reads, "Problem Solved." I was walking, holding my son's hand, when I noticed the T-shirts. I instinctively walked a little faster, hoping he wouldn't see them. I was not ready for him to know—and for me to explain—that many people think it is funny when men dislike or hurt their wives and girlfriends.

How did we get here? Today, we generally agree that straight people are those who "like" the other sex. This attraction is often understood to include mutual desire for intimate, romantic, love-based connection. These are such basic, defining features of contemporary heterosexuality that it can be tempting to imagine mutual desire and likability as the long-standing forces that have driven most heterosexual coupling. But historical evidence dispels us of this fantasy and helps us to understand why it is easy to find examples, on T-shirts and elsewhere, of men's simultaneous desire for and hatred of women—all wrapped together into

**Figures 2.1.** T-shirts sold by Crazy Shirts depicting straight men's heterosexual misery. (From CrazyShirts.com)

one dysfunctional sexual orientation. Across time and place, most forms of heterosexual coupling have been organized around men's ownership of women (their bodies, their work, their children) rather than their attraction to, or interest in, women. Women were men's property, slaves, and laborers, and women produced heirs to whom men could pass on their lineage and possessions.[1] Women were the people with whom men had procreative sex, and women of privilege (wealthy women, white women, women of high status) were sometimes perceived as delicate and virtuous, in need of men's protection and seduction (as in medieval and Victorian traditions of courtly and chivalrous love). But in none of these arrangements was "liking" women, or regarding them as men's most logical and beloved companions, a requirement in the way that contemporary straight culture now presumes—or at least strives. Liking women was hardly understood to be a fixed or defining feature of one's identity or "sexual orientation."

In the United States, the notion of *mutual likability* between women and men did not gain traction among American sexologists and social reformers until the late nineteenth and early twentieth centuries, just as the new concept of "the heterosexual" began to appear in medical textbooks. It took decades for both concepts—the idea that men and women should feel sexually and emotionally drawn to each other and that doing so meant that one was a heterosexual—to circulate widely enough that most Americans would have internalized them.[2] But by the late twentieth century, they converged to create a new relationship ideal, modern straightness, which represented a dramatic rupture in the way that men had related to women for centuries. This campaign for love-based heterosexual relationships was undoubtedly a positive development, as it created tension between men's violence against women, on the one hand, and the image of happy heterosexuality, on the other. But this transition from woman-as-degraded-subordinate to woman-as-worthy-of-deep-love was hardly smooth, nor is it complete. This unfinished transition, and its central role in the tragedy of heterosexuality, is where we will begin.

## Struggling for Straightness

The cultural expectation that men should like women, even as they are socialized into a culture that normalizes men's hatred of women, constitutes what I call straight culture's *misogyny paradox*. I first began thinking about the misogyny paradox when I read the extraordinary book *Women with Mustaches and Men without Beards: Gender and Sexual Anxieties of Iranian Modernity*, written by the feminist historian Afsaneh Najmabadi. Though Najmabadi's focus is on nineteenth-century Iran, her book is a case study with global and contemporary significance as it highlights the intersections between misogyny, heterosexuality, and imperialism. In a nutshell, Najmabadi argues that as the new concept of heterosexuality began to circulate in the nineteenth century,[3] Iranians resisted one of its defining principles—that men should feel love for, and desire companionship with, women. This idea was a "hard sell," Najmabadi explains, not only because it conflicted with long-standing beliefs about women's subordination and degraded status (how could men love their inferiors?) but also because most Iranians had lived in gender-segregated and homosocial (if not homoerotic) environments in which intimacy was reserved for people of the same sex.[4] Najmabadi further explains that even heterosexual *lust* was looked upon with suspicion by some Iranian commentators, because it stood to threaten men's patriarchal power: "if a woman can satisfy a man's desire, he may become enamored of her, develop an affection bordering on love, and consequently, become subordinate to her."[5] And yet, under the imperialist influence of Europe, where new ideas about the superiority of heterosexual romantic love and the pathology of homosociality were rapidly taking hold, the Iranian state launched a cultural campaign to encourage men and women to direct their affections toward each other. This represented a dramatic shift in the way that men's relationships with women were conceptualized, and it presented something of a paradox: "falling in love was what a man did with other men . . . [and] falling in love with women more often than not was unmanly," but modern heterosexuality compelled men to engage in precisely this unmanly act.[6]

Najmabadi's book drew my attention to two seemingly obvious but rarely acknowledged points: (1) modern notions of heterosexuality require men to feel love and affection for women, the very population they have dominated and dehumanized for centuries, and (2) this has caused many problems for straight people, who are struggling to transition from the trauma and legacy of misogyny to something more authentically "straight"—if by straightness, we mean authentic and noncoercive heterosexual love. While Najmabadi's focus was on Iran, there is evidence across the globe of men's resistance to loving their wives and other women sexual partners and of the historically and culturally varied manifestations of women's horrific subjugation by men in marriage.[7] The feminist scholar Gayle Rubin, for instance, famously offered a summary in her essay "The Traffic in Women," in which she details how economic and kinship systems around the world have relied on women being "given in marriage, taken in battle, exchanged for favors, sent as tribute, traded, bought, and sold" among husbands and male family members.[8] Some evidence of the misogyny paradox goes back centuries, such as scholarship on ancient Greece that documents that Athenian wives were regarded with contempt by their husbands and treated as servants within the family, while sexual relationships between adult men and boys were, in many cases, characterized by genuine affection and treated by Greek male society as a valuable method of preserving patriarchal power and strengthening male bonds.[9] Other evidence of the misogyny paradox comes from the eighteenth and nineteenth centuries, the same historical period of concern to Najmabadi. For instance, the historian Hanne Blank offers a telling account of heterosexuality in eighteenth- and nineteenth-century England and colonial America, citing the American preacher John Cotton's concern that so many men "despise and decry [wives] and call them a *necessary Evil*" and noting that, for several centuries, men who loved women were perceived as "effeminate" or "cunt-struck."[10]

The idea that men's romantic or even sexual interest in women is threatening to patriarchy, or "unmanly," may strike us as quite inconsistent with current understandings of heteromasculinity, yet there is ample evidence of the persistence of this view. Indeed, my own earlier research looked closely at the links between white heteromasculinity and expressions of disgust or resentment for the object of one's sexual desire—especially in the US military, in US fraternities, and in other male-dominated institutions in the United States.[11] In some of these institutions, girls and women are so degraded that for straight men to express enthusiastic interest in them, as desirable humans rather than as bitches, whores, and abject receptacles for penetration, is to subvert their own masculinity (now sometimes called being "henpecked" or "pussy-whipped").

Following the model set forth by Najmabadi and others, we now turn to the twentieth-century struggle for modern straightness in the United States and the concomitant emergence of a heterosexual-repair industry that capitalized on the difficulty of this project. Marriage experts recognized men's disinterest and violence toward women, and women's resentment and fear of men, as fundamental obstacles for straight relationships, and, consequently, they produced an industry designed to train men and women to like each other. But they were also committed to doing so without undermining men's authority or challenging the basic logic of the gender binary. These rehabilitative projects constitute the modern heterosexual-repair industry, an industry that capitalized on the difficult and unfinished transition from heterosexual coupling as a patriarchal contract to straightness as a relationship, and an identity, anchored in opposite-sex desire.

I focus on popular texts, accessible to lay women and men, that attempted to define healthy or normal heterosexual relationships and that also offered advice to readers about how to address conflicts in these relationships.[12] As our investigation of these texts will show, the emergence of straightness in the United States was not only entangled with misogyny and its effect on men's capacity to love women but also bound up with American racial projects. Eugenicist campaigns for white marital harmony profoundly shaped American heterosexuality through the twentieth century and into the present. Romantic marriage—and the forging of bonds between white men and women—was offered to white couples as a white-supremacist strategy during the early Jim Crow era and later offered to African Americans as a central pathway to membership in American "normality."[13] As we tour through American self-help and marriage education texts from the early twentieth century to the present, we will see how various experts—eugenicists, physicians, sexologists, social reformers (both Black and white), and psychologists—aggressively marketed heterosexual love to Americans, campaigned to make it appear more appealing than homosocial intimacies, and developed myriad techniques to both normalize and unravel the misogyny paradox. As they did this, they built both an industry and a culture out of the contradictions of straightness.

## Heterosexual Repulsion in the Early Twentieth Century

Investigating the writing of prominent early twentieth-century social reformers interested in sex and marriage uncovers two striking points about the development of modern heterosexuality. First, the earliest "self-help" books about modern marriage were almost exclusively written by proponents of the eugenics movement, a violent and ostensibly scientific project aimed at encouraging reproduction among people of good genetic stock and discouraging or preventing population growth among undesired populations.[14] The modern eugenics movement began in the United Kingdom in the early 1900s and subsequently traveled to the United States, where it was used to provide a justification for Jim Crow segregation, antimiscegenation laws, and the forced sterilization of Black and immigrant women. But the eugenics movement also had an agenda for white Americans, which was to address any obstacles, including men's violence against women, that might prevent the flourishing of white families. Eugenicist writers, often with the support of the Eugenics Publishing Company, produced several books designed to educate white readers about the benefits of friendly and harmonious marriage, thereby laying the foundation for a new heterosexual ideal.

A second point that we can glean from the content of these books is that making white marriages "happy" was an uphill battle. Eugenicists such as Havelock Ellis, Marie Stopes, William Robinson, and Harland Long made perfectly clear what they understood to be the marital status quo of the time: men and women commonly wished harm on each other, found each other disgusting, and were made utterly miserable by marriage. They made no pretense of their understanding that men's sexual orientation toward women was characterized, in part, by a desire to cause women pain. Writing in 1903, the British sexologist and eugenicist Havelock Ellis described men's "latent cruelty in courtship" and women's receptivity to pain and domination as core heterosexual impulses:

A certain pleasure in manifesting his power over a woman by inflicting pain upon her is an outcome and survival of the primitive process of courtship, and an almost or quite normal constituent of the sexual impulse in man. . . . In the normal well-balanced and well-conditioned man this constituent of the sexual impulse, when present, is always held in check. When the normal man inflicts, or feels the impulse to inflict, some degree of physical pain on the woman he loves he can scarcely be said to be moved by cruelty. He feels . . . that the pain he inflicts, or desires to inflict, is really part of his love, and . . . is not really resented by the woman on whom it is exercised. . . . The feminine line delights in submitting to that force, and even finds pleasure in a slight amount of pain. . . . We see, also, that these two groups of feelings are complementary. . . . What men are impelled to give, women love to receive.[15]

Men, in the eyes of the early sexologists like Ellis, were violent, driven by instinct, and largely uninterested in women's sexual pleasure. Ellis optimistically speculated that women were receptive to these qualities, as long as men's primitive impulses were sufficiently contained.

But other marriage experts were more worried. Many viewed men's violence against women as a structural conflict for heterosexuality because what women most needed, in order to experience marriage as a site of "love" rather than rape, was for men to gently guide them into a state of sexual receptivity. Taking this conflict (i.e., women's desire for sexual pleasure and men's lack of interest in providing it) as a starting point, the most popular sexology texts on love and marriage written in the early 1900s focused on "the scandal of female sexual ignorance, the dangers of wedding night trauma, and the necessity of [men's] preliminary wooing [of women]."[16] These were the principal concerns put forward in the incredibly influential and best-selling 1918 sex and marriage manual *Married Love*, for instance, written by Marie Stopes, a British botanist and proponent of eugenics and white women's rights. Popular in part due to its intensely romantic and hopeful approach to "love's mysteries," the book also pulls no punches about the tragic state of heterosexual marriage for many women, including new brides shocked and repelled by the revelation of their husbands' naked bodies or "driven to suicide and insanity" by "the horror of the first night of marriage."[17] Rape and trauma, Stopes implied, constituted many women's introduction to marriage. Such texts make evident that in the early twentieth-century imagination of (what we now call) heterosexuality, women were hardly expected to feel an easy or instinctive attraction to men or their bodies, nor were men expected to concern themselves with women's emotional or physical experiences of sex. Married couples, as these texts proclaimed, needed to *achieve* mutual attraction and affection through proper education about anatomy and natural sex differences, an education that could be provided by sexologists and physicians.

A distinctive and common feature of early twentieth-century marriage self-help texts is their concern with the problem of mutual physical repulsion by wives and husbands. Sexologists and physicians by their own accounts were very busy teaching women and men how to make their bodies, and heterosexual sex itself, less repellent. Stopes was worried about the "mental revolt and loathing" that wives may feel in reaction to their husbands' sexual violence;[18] Ellis warned of the "stage of apparent repulsion and passivity" that seemed to be a normal part of women's experience of sex with their husbands (a stage he believed would eventually give way to "active participation");[19] William Robinson, another early twentieth-century sexologist and author whom I discuss in more detail shortly, hoped that his marriage-advice manuals would address the "disgust," "deep hatred," and "desire for injury and revenge" that heterosexual couples felt for each other.[20]

If heterosexual, reproductive, married intercourse was a core organizing principle of American life in the twentieth century, how could it also be so disgusting and rage inducing? On women's end, the most obvious answer comes from sexologists' own accounts: marriage was a site of repeated rape and dehumanization of women by their husbands, a situation that women struggled to endure and survive. But even beyond the well-documented patriarchal violence of marriage were other contributing factors. Intercourse between white American men and women—even as it was the key to the eugenics project of passing on "superior blood" and the patriarchal project of securing women's free reproductive labor—was also a sin of the flesh. Puritan beliefs about sex as degrading and bodies as unclean were in widespread circulation in the United States at the turn of the century, casting heterosexual intercourse as "a mere matter of duty: to be permitted by sufferance; joyless, disgusting in itself; a something to be avoided, even in thought, other than it is a necessity for the continuance of the race."[21] Syphilis was also a public health crisis and a dark cloud hanging over American sexuality during the first decades of the twentieth century, with 10 to 15 percent of the US population estimated to have been infected and with whites claiming that African Americans carried higher rates of sexually transmitted diseases.[22] Added to this was the fact that before getting married, most white women and men had limited access to heteroeroticism or any significant experience with opposite-sex bodies, while opportunities for homosocial romance and affection were relatively unfettered, especially for women, given that these affections constituted neither "sex" (defined by the presence of penis and vagina) nor evidence of a stigmatized homosexual personhood, which had yet to fully take hold in the United States.[23]

Eugenicists set out, then, to help white women and men find each other's bodies less repellent and to situate medical science, "or right knowledge," as a legitimate alternative to mutual disgust, religious anxieties, and shame about sexual pleasure. A classic example in this vein is a book called *Married Life and Happiness; or, Love and Comfort in Marriage*, which was written in 1922 by Dr. William Robinson, a urologist at Bronx Hospital and an influential early birth-control advocate and eugenicist. Robinson was a prolific writer of early twentieth-century self-help books (he also wrote *Woman: Her Sex and Love Life*; *Sexual Problems of Today*; and *Sex Knowledge for Women and Girls*), and his writing offers us a remarkable diagnosis of the miseries of heterosexual marriage. In one passage in *Married Life and Happiness*, for instance,

Robinson refuted the claim that heterosexual marriage makes people happy or that women and men have been marrying for thousands of years and getting along just fine (presumably the argument made by his critics). He explained,

> Yes, [they have] gotten along, but how? Have you observed the disillu-sionments, the heartaches, the disappointments? Have you measured the disgust, the indifference, the resentment, the mutual ill-will, the deep ha-tred, the desire for injury and revenge? Have you estimated the amount of ill-health, the grief, the pain, the daily suffering, the nightly tossing and restlessness? Have you any idea of the number of neurotic wives and neurasthenic [irritable] husbands? . . . I assert and could readily prove that the lives of married couples, particularly married women, is not very different from, not much better than, life in prison.[24]

This was Robinson's description of heterosexual marriage in its natural state, unguided by the counsel of expert physicians. For Robinson, like his contemporaries, this misery and "deep hatred" were heterosexuality's default, yet he believed they could be ameliorated with proper sexual hygiene and premarital education about opposite-sex genital anatomy. Mirroring Ellis and Stopes, much of his analysis was focused on the trouble of getting men and women to genuinely want to provide sexual pleasure to each other, a desire that Robinson claimed could be culti-vated if couples knew how to make their bodies more appealing. Doing so required making sure that both parties do not have syphilis or other sexually transmitted infections, that men are not sexually impotent, and that both women and men receive full medical checkups and attend to anything off-putting (including scrotal hernias, hemorrhoids, constipa-tion, gas, rashes, acne, snoring, obesity, bad breath, vaginal odor, and foot odor). Similarly, the 1918 book *Womanhood and Marriage* by the nutritionist Bernarr Macfadden urged husbands to forbid their wives to drink coffee and tea or risk encountering a flatulent wife in bed.[25] Foreshadowing the twentieth-century explosion of soaping, douching, shaving, bleaching, and other hygiene products marketed to white women to promote gender and racial purity,[26] Robinson encouraged women to overcome any moral objections to wearing makeup, corsetry, and perfumes that could make their bodies more enticing.

Early twentieth-century physicians viewed heterosexual attraction as something of a gauntlet—there were so many ways that men's and women's bodies could fail to be attractive to the other sex, and hence, expert guidance and proper preparation were crucial to making heterosexuality functional. Exemplifying the common perception that heterosexual love and intimacy are learned rather than instinctive accomplishments, Dr. Harland William Long, writing for the Eugenics Publishing Company in 1919, spent several pages of the book *Sane Sex Life and Sane Sex Living* asserting that young couples will rarely ever experience sexual success without the supervision of a knowledgeable medical professional to guide them at each step. Of particular concern to Long was the way that husbands' rape of their wives appeared to be the wedding-night default and that this formative sexual assault stood to ruin marriages from their outset. Speaking to other physicians and sexologists in the foreword to the book, he contends, "Many a newlywed couple have wrecked the possibility of happiness of a life time on their 'honey-moon trip'; and it is a matter of common knowledge to the members of our profession that the great majority of brides are practically raped on entrance into the married relation. Further than this, we all know that these things are as they are chiefly because of ignorance of the parties concerned."[27] Long goes to great lengths to renounce marital rape and inform his readers about the value of approaching intercourse slowly, stroking the vulva before penetration, prioritizing women's orgasm, and embracing masturbation in moderation. Exemplifying what would become a trend in the marriage self-help industry, Long advised that newlyweds read his book together in the hope that they could develop some communication skills and come to some informed agreements about what constitutes "sane sex." Yet he also warned his fellow physicians that "this book can only be used professionally. . . .

It needs the guiding hand of an expert physician to insure its reaching only those who can be benefited by its reading" (Long confessed to mixed results with couples who were already years into sexually violent marriages).[28]

While white physicians described nonviolent, affectionate heterosexuality as a difficult but necessary component of the stability of white families, African American physicians and social reformers declared it a social and political right—one that Black men and women had been denied under the conditions of slavery and poverty and that held the key to African American survival, freedom, and respectability.[29] Marriage, and the ability to choose and remain with one's sexual and familial partners more generally, was of paramount importance to former slaves and their descendants following centuries of brutal rupture of enslaved families at the hands of white slave owners. As the legal scholar Katherine Franke has shown, many abolitionists in the United States viewed marriage as central to the experience of emancipation, thereby laying the groundwork for marriage to be reconceptualized as a freedom, rather than an economic obligation or necessity, in the twentieth-century American imagination.[30] Although white male reformers continued to focus on constraining women's sexual autonomy and encouraging conformity to Victorian ideas about women as temperamentally suited to motherhood and domestic pursuits, African American reformers focused on the ways Black sexual respectability was best achieved through Black women's freedom of choice. Departing from the majority of white social hygienists' opposition to birth control, for instance, Dr. Charles Roman, an African American physician and author, proclaimed that African American women should be provided with "intellectual and moral" instruction about their options and then left "the freedom and responsibility of a decision."[31] First-wave feminists, both Black and white, *also* advocated for modern, companionate marriage in the hope that women would experience less misogyny, and greater equity and fulfillment, in what continued to be a legally sanctioned domain of women's sexual and domestic servitude.[32] In the early twentieth century, the work of "making marriage modern," or less damaged by men's violence, was a widely embraced progressive value.[33]

But the American construction of modern heterosexuality was inseparable from white-supremacist gender norms. White male social reformers, who possessed far greater power and authority than civil rights and feminist activists, defined healthy heterosexual marriage in their own image and according to their own interests. Marital rape may have been discouraged by white male marriage experts of the twentieth century, but their emphasis on men's entitlement to women's emotional and reproductive labor, and women's ostensibly innate vulnerability, virtue, and tendency toward self-sacrifice, ensured that modern heterosexuality served the interests of white supremacy. As the Black feminist scholar Hortense Spillers illuminates, whites treated Black people with such dehumanizing, "ungendering" brutality during slavery and its aftermath that whites effectively barred Black men from the kind of patriarchal power that constituted masculinity and Black women from the kind of purity and fragility that constituted femininity.[34] Slavery and anti-Black racism positioned Black people outside the boundaries of a white gender binary, as threats not only to white ideas about normative masculinity and femininity but also to white men and women's unity with each other.[35] Illustrating the inseparability of modern heterosexuality and white supremacy, many early white feminists based their arguments for nonviolent marriage and women's rights on the claim that bringing white women closer to equality with their husbands would ensure that white people remained a united front against Black civil rights. If white men forged egalitarian, companionate bonds with white women, they argued, then white women would offer race loyalty in return.

In sum, eugenicists, sexologists, and social reformers of the early twentieth century ushered in three concepts that would become enduring features of the heterosexual-repair industry. First, they exposed the ubiquity of violence and mutual loathing in heterosexual relationships but also reassured their readers that these were natural impulses in need of simple management. Rape could be curtailed by sexual and anatomical education. Mutual disgust could be diminished by better hygiene and beautification of the body. Communication between the sexes could be improved if couples read and discussed, together, the right marital literature written by knowledgeable guides. Second, they secured their own role and the role of expert white professionals more generally—physicians, sexologists, and later, psychologists—in defining modern heterosexuality and repairing heterosexual problems. By naming men's and women's ignorance of the unique temperament and anatomy of the opposite sex as the source of straight couples' problems—rather than, say, patriarchy and white supremacy—early promoters of modern heteroromance introduced self-help projects, guided by marriage experts, as the new normal. Heterosexual desire and mutual likability did not come naturally, they acknowledged, but could be cultivated with the proper tools. Last, they accepted the premise that women and men often found each other's bodies undesirable and hence advocated for the consumption of beauty products that help stimulate opposite-sex desire. Laying the foundation for the midcentury explosion of beauty interventions targeted to women attempting to appear "fresh" and "lovely" for their husbands while laboring at home, eugenicist advocates for hygienic and modern marriage offered soaps, perfumes, makeup, douching, and other consumer goods as keys to happy heterosexuality. They made explicit that heterosexual marriage was no longer a labor contract in which both parties showed up "as is" but an ongoing affective project requiring access to precise tools and information that would build mutual affection.

Each of these interventions set the stage for straight culture's emergence as the romantic arm of misogyny, wherein the delicate coexistence of hate and love, the slap and the kiss, would come to represent the heteroerotic. But this era also initiated straight culture as a gendered mode of consumption in which the purchase of beauty products and relationship advice were vital to maintaining this delicate balance.

## Heterosexual Disinterest at Midcentury

Oh, there is nothing quite so explicit as the sexism of 1950s marriage manuals! By midcentury, marriage experts had moved beyond the problem of men's and women's disgusting and unhygienic bodies and directed their attention to women's annoying personalities—or men's irritation with listening to their wives speak and, in many cases, their indignation about their wives' disappointing cooking.[36] As the Reverend Alfred Henry Tyrer proclaimed in his 1951 book *Sex Satisfaction and Happy Marriage*, "The happiness of homes is destroyed more frequently by the habit of nagging than any other one thing. . . . The word home may be defined as 'a place where a man goes after business hours to be nagged at.' A man may stand this sort of thing for a long time, but the chances are against his standing it permanently."[37] Midcentury marriage experts' focus on men's irritation, or husbands and wives "not getting along," signals the popularity of mutual likability as a cultural aspiration in this period; marital love and happiness were now common expectations that could produce dissonance for married couples when they did not appreciate each other's company. To resolve heterosexual conflicts, women were counseled to be submissive and lovely, to put their husbands' concerns first, and to keep both themselves and their homes quiet and beautiful—and the source of delicious, homemade meals. The figure of the happy housewife was almost always embodied by white women in 1950s popular culture, with African American women nearly invisible in mainstream media or portrayed as servants and domestic workers. But we can glean much about the construction of 1950s and 1960s Black heterosexuality from accounts of sexism within the civil rights and Black Power movements, in which many women were sexually harassed, expected to follow men's leadership, and asked to devote themselves to men's concerns and public visibility.[38] In a telling and historically significant example, Black women organizers and strategists were not allowed to speak onstage during the 1963 March on Washington, despite being central to the very planning of the event.[39]

Numerous social, economic, and political trends shaped modern American heterosexuality during this period. The eugenics movement, associated with Nazi Germany and the Holocaust, fell out of favor in the United States by the 1950s, while the disciplines of psychology and sociology—with their focus on family roles and societal problems, respectively—had gained momentum and institutional recognition. As psychology found its way into popular culture, so too did the emergent concept of "gender roles"—a term popularized in the 1950s by the psychologist John Money to give name to normative male and female differences in "general mannerisms, deportment and demeanor; play preferences and recreational interests; spontaneous topics of talk; . . . content of dreams, daydreams and fantasies; . . . and erotic practices."[40] Technologies of the home, such as electric kitchen appliances and time-saving household gadgets of all kinds, also proliferated during the postwar economic boom, with advertisers speaking directly to women consumers about how these products would keep husbands happy and hence themselves. All of these developments provided the backdrop for midcentury marriage-advice frameworks.

Midcentury gender ideology looked remarkably as it had in the decades prior: modesty, caretaking, and domesticity were presumably women's realms, while emotional repression, restrained lust, autonomy, and competition became even more strongly tied to masculinity. Despite the entrenchment of a rigid gender binary constructing women and men as opposite human types with little foundation for mutual interest, 1950s gender ideology required that women, if not also men, strive for romantic love—an endeavor resulting in an endless stream of advice books, magazine columns, and educational films aimed at helping wives produce happy marriages.[41] In particular, the tension between the expectation of heterosexual love and men's unapologetic disinterest in conversation with their wives produced a demand among women readers for advice on how to cultivate their husbands' affection. For instance, Dr. Edward Podolsky's 1947 book *Sex Today in Wedded Life: A Doctors Confidential Advice* includes a list of "10 Commandments for Wives":

1. Don't bother your husband with petty troubles and complaints when he comes home from work.
2. Be a good listener. Let him tell you his troubles; yours will seem trivial in comparison.
3. Remember your most important job is to build up and maintain his ego (which gets bruised plenty in business). Morale is a woman's business.
4. Let him relax before dinner, and discuss family problems after the "inner man" has been satisfied.
5. Always remember he's a male and marital relations promote harmony. Have sane views about sex.
6. No man likes a wife who is always tired out. Conserve your energy so you can give him the companionship he craves.
7. Never hold up your husband to ridicule in the presence of others. If you must criticize, do so privately and without anger.
8. Remember a man is only a grown-up boy. He needs mothering and enjoys it if not piled on too thick.
9. Don't live beyond your means, or add to your husband's financial burdens.
10. Don't try to boss him around. Let him think he wears the pants.[42]

As with Podolsky's book, much of the marital advice marketed to women at this time attempted to normalize a midcentury gender binary in which men were busy, important, and indifferent to their wives, whose own lives were "trivial in comparison." Midcentury self-help books urged women to feel sympathy for men, who held the weight of the heartless world on their shoulders. Today, feminists have thankfully reframed this claim as an example of "fragile masculinity," but through much of the twentieth century, self-help books made clear to women that they should take men's stress very seriously if they wished to remain married. Being employed in the world of "business" was enough to push a man over the edge. Accommodating wives should be mindful of household sounds, including their children's voices, be prompt with dinner, and avoid subjecting their husbands to any unwanted conversation. Women frustrated with this state of affairs could turn to marriage-advice books written by authoritative men, such as Podolsky and Tyrer, but most of these texts would simply affirm the gendered lopsidedness of heterosexual love: women are to appreciate men's humanity—their ideas, triumphs, and vulnerabilities—though they should hardly expect men to offer the same in return.

Echoing this emphasis on men's important pursuits and women's devotion to their husbands, the Black feminist Michelle Wallace argues that the midcentury was time of increased patriarchal control of Black women resulting from Black men's demands for power and manhood during the civil rights movement. Wallace notes that while Black women were in many ways more engaged in economic and political life than white women of this era were, they were nonetheless expected to submit to the authority of their male partners, to center men's interests over their own in ways that resembled the gender dynamics of white heterosexuality. A Black woman's contribution to the struggle for racial justice was her intimate care of her man (cleaning and cooking for him, raising his children, boosting his morale) and her agreement to "keep her mouth shut" and "stand by silently as he became a 'man.'"[43] Wallace explains, "Day to day, these women, like most women, devoted their energies to their husbands and children. When they found time, they worked on reforms in education, medicine, housing, and their communities through their organizations and churches. Little did they know that one day their activities would be used as proof that the black woman has never known her place and has mightily battled the black man for his male prerogative as head of the household."[44] The nexus of white supremacy and patriarchy positioned Black women in a complex bind: the work they did to address racial oppression in their communities was urgently needed but was also viewed as a threat to Black men's leadership and self-worth. The 1965 government-sponsored report titled *The Negro Family*, authored by the white sociologist Patrick Moynihan, incited much of this fear about Black women's autonomy and leadership. It was Black women's failure to be sufficiently domestic and submissive to Black men, Moynihan argued, that was to blame for poverty and violence in Black "ghettos."[45] Unlike for white women, Black wives' loyalty to their husbands took center stage in a national discussion about race and poverty. In the eyes of Moynihan and his many supporters, the very future of Black communities rested on Black women's capacity to be compliant housewives.

Unlike in the early twentieth century, when healthy heterosexuality was the responsibility of both men and women (i.e., marital-hygiene manuals were given to both parties by their physicians), at midcentury it was women, the managers of men's morale and the stewards of household and community happiness, who became responsible for addressing the contradictions of heterosexuality. As the eugenicists had introduced earlier, a primary strategy that women could use was to make their bodies more physically desirable. Print ads from the 1940s–1960s instructed women on the importance of being hardworking, happy housewives while also keeping their bodies "fresh" and sexually appealing to their husbands: Lysol promised that a wife "can keep her husband and herself eager, happy married lovers" by douching with Lysol to ensure good feminine hygiene (a 1950s code for contraception, according to some historians).[46] An ad for Kellogg's PEP vitamins promised wives that they could cook and clean and still "look cute" for their husbands if they took the right vitamins. An ad for LUX Stockings warned married women not to neglect their stockings just because they were married: "husbands admire wives who keep their stockings perfect." An ad for the Wear Ever Pressure Cooker assured women that they could "look pretty and daisy fresh, yet serve the tastiest food he ever ate!" A 1952 Edison Electric commercial showed a teenage girl seducing her older brother's friend by listening adoringly and complimenting his intelligence as he explains the mechanical function of kitchen appliances.[47] Ads marketed to African American women in *Ebony* magazine reflected these same themes (e.g., Lysol's "Be Confident!" vaginal-douche campaign appeared in white magazines with a photo of a white model and in *Ebony* with a photo of a

Black model) but also included numerous ads for hair-straightening and skin-lightening products that promised to make Black women "lighter and lovelier" (and that depicted smiling Black women cradled by adoring Black men).[48] Advertisers skillfully connected their products—from cosmetics to electric dishwashers—to the project of heterosexual repair by depicting images of happy heterosexual couples seemingly unburdened by men's violence or fragility.

But the ads also capitalized on men's still tenuous and largely transactional attachment to women. If wives were not careful about their appearance and caretaking responsibilities, they were in danger of losing their husbands or suffering their wrath. This looming threat became a core feature of straight culture, one regularly depicted in music, television, and film of the 1950s and 1960s. The tenuousness, or temporariness, of heterosexual attraction is expressed quite clearly, for instance, in Frank Sinatra's 1964 song "Wives and Lovers": "Hey, little girl, comb your hair, fix your makeup. Soon he will open the door. Don't think because there's a ring on your finger, you needn't try any more. . . . I'm warning you." Phenomenally successful 1950s television programs like *The Honeymooners* and *I Love Lucy* normalized heterosexual marriage as a site of mutual dislike, manipulation, and men's violence against women (while Ralph threatened to hit Alice in nearly every episode of *The Honeymooners*, Ricky actually spanked Lucy until she cried in two episodes of *I Love Lucy*. Similarly, an image of a husband spanking his wife was also used in Chase & Sanborn Coffee advertisements of the 1950s to depict the consequences of women buying stale coffee).[49] Husbands' dislike of their wives, and the depiction of marriage as a trap or a prison for men, was a basic ingredient of the comedic formula of these shows (one that would appear again, with great success, in the hit 1990s sitcom *Married with Children*). Wives like Lucy Ricardo, Ethel Mertz, and Alice Kramden not only were nags and/or spendthrifts in the eyes of their husbands but also were haggard and sexually unappealing compared with younger, unmarried women. But viewers were led to believe that, despite all of this conflict and dissatisfaction, husbands like

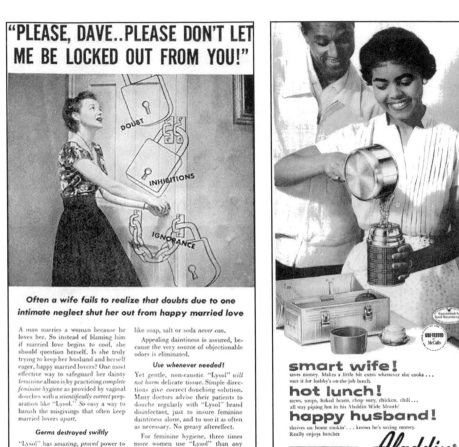

# "PLEASE, DAVE..PLEASE DON'T LET ME BE LOCKED OUT FROM YOU!"

DOUBT

INHIBITIONS

IGNORANCE

**Often a wife fails to realize that doubts due to one intimate neglect shut her out from happy married love**

A man marries a woman because he loves her. So instead of blaming him if married love begins to cool, she should question herself. Is she truly trying to keep her husband and herself eager, happy married lovers? One most effective way to safeguard her dainty *feminine allure* is by practicing *complete feminine hygiene* as provided by vaginal douches with a *scientifically correct* preparation like "Lysol." So easy a way to banish the misgivings that often keep married lovers *apart*.

**Germs destroyed swiftly**

"Lysol" has amazing, *proved* power to kill germ-life on contact . . . truly cleanses the vaginal canal even in the presence of mucous matter. Thus "Lysol" *acts* in a way that makeshifts

like soap, salt or soda *never can*.

Appealing daintiness is assured, because the very source of objectionable odors is eliminated.

**Use whenever needed!**

Yet gentle, non-caustic "Lysol" *will not harm* delicate tissue. Simple directions give correct douching solution. Many doctors advise their patients to douche regularly with "Lysol" brand disinfectant, just to insure feminine daintiness alone, and to use it as often as necessary. No greasy aftereffect.

For feminine hygiene, three times more women use "Lysol" than any other liquid preparation. No other is more reliable. You, too, can rely on "Lysol" to help protect your married happiness . . . keep you desirable!

**For complete Feminine Hygiene rely on . . .**

"*Lysol*"
Brand Disinfectant

**A Concentrated Germ-Killer**

**smart wife!**
saves money. Makes a little bit extra whenever she cooks . . . uses it for hubby's on-the-job lunch.

**hot lunch!**
stews, soups, baked beans, chop suey, chicken, chili . . . all stay piping hot in his Aladdin Wide Mouth!

**happy husband!**
thrives on home cookin'. . . knows he's saving money. Really enjoys lunches

*Aladdin*®

BEST-BUY® WIDE MOUTH VACUUM BOTTLES

Featuring the famous heat-and-flavor sealing LOX-ON® stoppers, threadless dishtype cup-cap, 10 oz., Pint, Quart sizes. Performance guaranteed.

WORKMEN'S LUNCH KITS, TOO

Rust-proof, scratch-proof, light-weight Lifetime Aluminum: or heavy-gauge embossed black steel. With Aladdin pint vacuum bottles.

*T.M.

*at your nearby hardware, drug, variety, department store or supermarket*

42

**Figures 2.2.** Midcentury advertisements linking marital happiness to vaginal douching, good cooking, and skin bleaching (*see facing page*), respectively.

*I want these roses to see how lovely you are*

*Bob*

# Wonderful things happen

## when your complexion is clear, bright, Nadinola-light

**Give romance a chance!** Don't let a dull, dark complexion deprive you of popularity. Don't let oiliness, big pores, blackheads cheat you of charm. Chase away those bad-complexion blues with NADINOLA Bleaching Cream. Nothing—absolutely *nothing*—will improve your skin faster, in more different ways!

**Contains wonder-working A-M!** This remarkable medicated ingredient of NADINOLA works deep down *within* the skin to brighten and lighten it, combat blackheads

and externally caused pimples. Soon your skin feels cleansed and cleared, smoother and softer, glowing and glamorous.

**Effective but oh, so gentle!** NADINOLA acts so *positively* yet is so *kind* to your skin that we guarantee you will be delighted with its results. There are two types—one for oily skin and the other for dry skin. Choose the type that is right for *you*. Buy it confidently, use it happily. NADINOLA, Paris, Tennessee.

# NADINOLA

## BLEACHING CREAM

*Just one jar will make your complexion brighter, clearer, lighter and lovelier.*

**FOR OILY SKIN**
Nadinola Deluxe is
non-oily. Brightens skin,
lessens shine at the
same time. 75c to $2

**FOR DRY SKIN**
The original Nadinola
is enriched with fine
cosmetic oils to relieve
dryness. 25c to $1.25

Ricky Ricardo, Fred Mertz, and Ralph Kramden were ultimately good men who loved their wives—thereby inaugurating what would become a long television tradition of braiding together marital misogyny, or men's aversion to their wives, with heterosexual love.

To the extent that self-help was targeted to men during this period, it largely took the form of media that could help men *escape* women's expectations of romantic love. *Playboy* magazine, founded in 1953, spoke directly to married men's nostalgia for bachelorhood and their craving for homosocial environments, encouraging men to seek time away from their wives.[50] *Playboy* offered men sexual images of women they could eroticize without any expectation of love or friendship, but it also created a virtual community of men—a space where real love and friendship, the kind experienced among men, could at least be approximated on the page, between a sympathetic male columnist and his male reader. Writing about *Playboy* magazine as an exemplar of commercial men's culture more broadly, the social critic Varda Burstyn has argued that "instead of encouraging an equal division of paid and unpaid work to resolve the problems between men and women within the family in late capitalist society, commercial men's cultures—both erotic and sporting—proposed ways to keep men's economic, social, and libidinal energies tied up away from home, in nonprocreational sex with young women, [and] in homosocial relations with men."[51] Serving a similar function, fraternal clubs and stag parties were also popular environments for heterosexual men to seek refuge from the companionship of their wives and find it, temporarily, with one another instead. Such spaces arguably laid the groundwork for a later male space—the 1990s "man cave"—that would integrate the site of men's escape into the darker recesses (the basement, the garage) of the family home, though now isolated from other men. As the gender theorist Paul Preciado asserts, 1950s fantasy spaces merging the corporate, the domestic, and the pornographic—bachelor pads, the Playboy penthouse, Hugh Hefner's mansion—signaled the ways that modern masculinity would be marked by a longing to escape the space of married life.[52] But ultimately, because these forms of homosociality were virtual or fleeting—forged among Playboy's far-flung readership or at periodic stag parties—they failed to produce real-life or sustained connections among men, arguably intensifying men's reliance on women to meet their emotional needs, in person, in the twentieth century.

Although midcentury representations of heterosexuality very often told the story of wives struggling to please husbands who did not seem to like them very much, some marriage-education films of the time showed couples "working it out" or portrayed modern marriage as wholesome and mutually fulfilling, akin to the idealized representation of marriage in the 1957 television show *Leave It to Beaver*. For instance, the male narrator in a film series titled *Marriage Today*, based on Henry Bowman's 1948 book *Marriage for Moderns*, responds directly to men's negative perceptions about women and marriage, explaining that wives can be interesting, independent people. In one scene, viewers learn that "Phyllis met Chad at the university in a math course. She got the better grades. Now he's an engineer, and she's a housewife." The narrator explains that while Phyllis used to engage in "useful and interesting" work in a laboratory, it was her desire for children that made her freely choose to marry. ("Freedom of choice," the narrator asserts at this moment in the film, "it's a modern privilege and a modern responsibility.") In another vignette, the narrator illustrates women's personhood through the story of Katherine, a schoolteacher and a wife: "Just as she believes that a child is a person and entitled to respect and consideration, Katherine Hartford, another wife in our town, believes a married woman is a person too. Katherine is modern. . . . For her, the husband is not a master, nor the wife a slave. She doesn't think the children in her classroom are inferior to her, and she doesn't think of herself as in any way inferior to [her husband] Frank. Different, yes—as every man is from every woman, . . . but one isn't better than the other."[53] Here, modern marriage is characterized by the recognition of a wife's personhood, just as one recognizes the personhood of a child. As with the child, this discursive recognition of personhood had no effect on the long-standing structural conditions that assigned greater value and freedom to one person over the other—whether adult-child or husband-wife. Instead, 1950s marriage-education films offered straight women a mechanism to imagine that their conformity and submission had nothing to do with the patriarchal foundation of heterosexual marriage itself but were instead individual acts of self-expression. Representing what would become a persistent theme in the American heterosexual-repair industry, such films obscured the coercive pipeline that tracked women into heterosexual marriage, motherhood, and free labor by situating the figure of the wife within a seemingly feminist discourse about women's "freedom to choose."

In a relatively progressive marriage propaganda film of the 1950s, *Who's the Boss? Married Life, Learning to Live Together*, a wife named Virginia and her husband, Mike, are both publishing professionals who argue constantly and compete for power in their marriage until these issues are resolved when the couple has two children. As a mother, Virginia works only "once in a while," and Mike helps out with the parenting. While these modest gestures at gender equity, along with the depiction of a dual-profession marriage, stand out among 1950s marriage-education films, I mention *Who's the Boss?* here because of a different feature of the film. The film introduces without much comment a heterosexual strategy that would become a centerpiece of John Gray's advice four decades later in the 1990s self-help classic *Men Are from Mars, Women Are from Venus*. In the absence of clear and direct communication, Virginia and Mike are shown in the film using obscure nonverbal signals to communicate their needs to each other. The male narrator of *Who's the Boss?* tells viewers that Virginia learns to wear her apron backward to communicate to her husband that he should "take it easy" because she "needs tender loving care" that night. The narrator then explains that Mike spins his hat on his finger to signal to Virginia that "it's one of those days when a fella needs a friend." Whether these gestures hint at the couples' desire for sex or just physical closeness is unclear (to me anyway), but they exemplify the kind of coy communication game that would later become a popular therapeutic recommendation for troubled straight couples in the 1990s.

In sum, midcentury representations of marriage doubled down on earlier themes of opposite-sex disinterest and resentment by suggesting to women that not only their bodies but also their personalities needed to be carefully managed in order to produce happy heterosexuality. As experts elaborated their expectations of the good wife, women's submission and self-sacrifice became central ingredients of straight culture, with women warned about what they must give up in order to "keep their men" (the list of sacrifices included their jobs and interests, their desire for adult conversation, their selfhood). Straight culture was also marked by men's fragility and irritation, their pervasive sense of burden, loss, and entrapment. Men were encouraged to fantasize about freedom from emotional intimacy with women or to dream of a life characterized by diminished heterosexual demands (i.e., bachelorhood) and expanded homosocial bonds (the company of men). Of particular significance to my analysis of the heterosexual-repair industry is the fact that midcentury advertisers learned to capitalize on the tragedy of heterosexuality by creating ads that played on men's desire for freedom and power over women and women's desire to be attractive and interesting to their husbands.[54] Marketers recognized that women had to work to achieve and sustain men's transitory satisfaction with heterosexual marriage or face the threat of abandonment and economic insecurity. Women's subordination and precarity within heterosexual relationships gave marketers a phenomenally effective "hook" for reaching straight women consumers, a hook that would continue to animate the heterosexual-repair industry into the next several decades.[55]

## Heterosexual Misery in the Late Twentieth Century

Influenced by second-wave feminist critiques of gender inequality in heterosexual relationships, the late twentieth century was witness to dramatic shifts in the representation of straight culture. Popular 1980s family sitcoms, such as *Family Ties* and *The Cosby Show*, depicted feminist heterosexual relationships in which wives were successful professionals, husbands were adoring and egalitarian, and marriages were unions of best friends. By the late 1990s, the hit sitcom *Friends* pushed the fantasy of happy heterosexuality even further, depicting a seemingly postfeminist urban landscape in which single young women and men forged enduring friendships with each other and later became married soul mates. Wedding- and baby-themed reality television programs were also phenomenally popular with straight women viewers during the 1990s, a fact that the cultural studies scholar Jennifer Maher attributes to the disappointment of heterosexual rituals and institutions in women's actual lives.[56] For Maher, the gap between the fantasy and the lived experience of heterosexuality (or the reality of married life and parenting *after* the wedding day and baby's birth) left women disappointed and wanting more, a craving that was soothed by watching the fantasy reenacted on screen over and over again.

A review of the widely popular marital self-help books published during this period supports Maher's hypothesis. In 1985, the breakout book *Women Who Love Too Much* by Robin Norwood, a number-one *New York Times* best seller, announced that millions of women around the globe—"in the United States, . . . China and Brazil, France and Finland, Ireland and Israel, Saudi Arabia and Serbia"—had become addicted to unstable, immature, angry, cold, and abusive men and had found solace in Norwood's writing.[57] Women who loved too much were "redeeming men through the gift of their selfless, perfect, all-accepting love" and would do almost anything for men's company and approval.[58] Drawing heavily from twelve-step, addiction-focused approaches to codependency, Norwood argued that women needed to learn to validate themselves and stop trying to change men to meet their needs. In a similar vein, the spiritual writer Iyanla Vanzant—a protégé of Oprah Winfrey's—also argued in her number-one best-selling book *In the Meantime: Finding Yourself and the Love You Want* that women need to undertake a complete spiritual and emotional inventory in order to ready themselves for men's love.[59] Promoting a sentiment that had been, and would continue to be, circulated among straight women for decades, Vanzant told women readers—her primary audience—that they must first learn to truly love themselves, and to know that they are complete without a male partner, before they can receive love from men.

Another number-one *New York Times* best seller from this era, *Men Who Hate Women and the Women Who Love Them*, by the psychologist Susan Forward and published in 1986, took a different and more feminist approach by naming misogyny, rather than codependency or lack of self-love, as the main dysfunction of the tragedy of heterosexuality. The book boldly demonstrated that misogyny was a widespread problem, characterized by men who controlled, devalued, yelled at, threatened, blamed, and frightened the women they claimed to love. These men flew into rages and acted like "hungry, demanding infants" who expected women to be "a never-ending source of total, all-giving love, adoration, concern, approval and nurturing."[60] In a particularly striking passage that echoes William Robinson's account of heterosexual marriages seventy years prior, Forward acknowledged that readers may wonder about her use of the word "hatred" to describe many heterosexual relationships: "I realize that my use of the word *hatred* in the context of an intimate relationship is both explosive and controversial. . . . But it is the only word that sufficiently describes the combination of hostility, aggression, contempt, and cruelty that the misogynist exhibits in his behavior toward his partner."[61] Also echoing Afsaneh Najmabadi's assertion that nineteenth-century Iranian men recoiled at the idea of loving women because doing so might give women power, Forward explained that men's abuse of women is driven by fear that "if he loves a woman, she will then have the power to hurt him, to deprive him, to engulf him, to abandon him."[62] Despite her sharp analysis of misogyny, Forward, like Norwood, ultimately placed responsibility for change in individual women's hands. Women needed to stop normalizing men's abuse, set limits on what they would tolerate, and learn to assert their own needs.

This turn toward women's self-worth and autonomy is inseparable from late twentieth-century "postfeminist" messages about straight women's sexuality and consumer practices as their sources of power.

Late-1990s television shows like the phenomenally popular HBO series *Sex and the City* (based on Candace Bushnell's 1997 book by the same name) linked "girl power" to straight women's access to wealth and consumer objects, desirability and casual sex. Straight Black women, already constructed as excessively sexual, bold, and independent by white commentators like Patrick Moynihan, represented the extreme end of women's sexual freedom—or their capacity to be unapologetic freaks and bitches—in the white-supremacist imagination. Citing the rise to stardom of popular women performers like Jennifer Lopez, Beyoncé, and Missy Elliott, the Black feminist scholar Patricia Hill Collins describes this period as a time in which Black and Brown women "were convinced to perceive themselves solely in terms of the value of their booties in marketplace relations" and in which the long-standing white-supremacist obsession with Black and Brown body parts and sexual deviance began to converge with neoliberal notions of freedom.[63] At the same time that best-selling self-help books of the era signaled that straight relationships were characterized by the misogyny of husbands and the lack of self-love and self-confidence of wives, straight women were offered a new corporate-mediated and racially appropriative discourse that emphasized casual sex—and not feminist critique, which was considered passé by many women during this era—as one way of managing the disappointments of heterosexuality.

Another exceedingly popular response to the heterosexual tragedy was simply to *normalize* it, and no book was as successful at spreading the word that men and women do not like each other as the psychologist John Gray's 1992 book *Men Are from Mars, Women Are from Venus.* Gray's book sold over fifty million copies and was the best-selling nonfiction book during the entire decade of the 1990s, facts that are tremendously significant given the book's central and now familiar message: men and women are so different, so at odds, that they might as well be from two different planets. Gray confirmed for millions of readers that men and women do not naturally like or respect each other, and therefore they would need to learn to "fake it" for the sake of their relationships. While

**Figure 2.3.** John Gray speaks to an audience of women.

this may seem depressing, Gray reassured readers that heterosexual alien-ation is perfectly natural and nothing to worry about. If straight couples could learn to fake connection well enough, they might also learn to meet each other's needs and become authentically connected. What does this faking entail? Gray told men that even though they may be bored and irritated when their wives want to speak to them, it is men's duty to listen and pretend to be interested because women naturally thrive on commu-nication and connection. Gray told women that even though they resent their husbands for being adults who could not clean up after themselves without being reminded, they must still lovingly remind husbands to do their chores and, more importantly, express gratitude when they do, be-cause men thrive on affirmation. He explained that men should be left alone to watch football in their dens and basements (their "caves") while women take care of the children and the house because retreating to the cave is a perfectly normal, ancient Martian tradition. Women should be bought flowers and reassured that they are loved, because even though Martians find these acts pointless, they are ancient Venutian traditions that make women both happy and receptive to sex.

It would be difficult to overstate the significance of *Men Are from Mars, Women Are from Venus* as a self-help phenomenon that renormalized heterosexual misery for a new generation. This book—whose central message was that women and men naturally find each other difficult to tolerate—spawned six follow-up books (*Venus and Mars on a Date, Venus and Mars in the Bedroom, Venus and Mars Starting Over*, and *Why Mars and Venus Collide*) and was published in Korean, Chinese, Japanese, Spanish, Indonesian, Arabic, Sinhalese, and French. As others have noted, the book's gender essentialism provided a reassuring counterpoint to the mounting feminist evidence that gender roles are socially constructed and therefore mutable, and it provided readers an alternative to the slow and difficult work of feminist social change.[64] In this vein, John Gray offered a blueprint for a widely adopted, late-modern "patriarchal bargain," to use the feminist political-economist Deniz Kandiyoti's term, wherein women who perceive feminism to threaten their symbolic capital, safety, or respectability could choose instead a set of private, interpersonal negotiations (such as performing dramatic displays of gratitude when male partners engage in equitable behavior).[65] Drawing from numerous global examples, Kandioyoti illustrates that many women "would rather adopt interpersonal strategies that maximize their security through manipulation of the affections of their sons and husband" rather than resist in ways that might deem them bad women—such as engaging in collective, public support for the redistribution of gendered power.[66] Playing right into this patriarchal bargain, *Men Are from Mars, Women Are from Venus* offered a contemporary menu of the emotional compromises and manipulations that women, and men, could take up when feminism seemed untenable. The book opened the floodgates for a host of others that would take up the same strategy.

For instance, a similarly successful 1990s phenomenon was the *New York Times* number-one best seller *The 5 Love Languages* by Gary Chapman, which sold over ten million copies and continues to be a top-selling marriage-advice manual despite being published in 1992. Though

*The 5 Love Languages* seemed at first blush to be a gender-neutral exploration of the different ways that partners express and receive love, Chapman's gendered language and examples made clear that the book's intended audience was Venutians—or ungrateful, disappointed, or nagging wives—and that Martians, or husbands who just want to be praised and then left alone, were the intended beneficiaries. In one example that Chapman discussed at length, a wife is frustrated because she had been asking her husband to paint the bedroom for nine months and he still hadn't done it. Chapman's advice was for her to compliment her husband on anything that he actually *does* do. Chapman told her never to mention the painting job again and then stated,

> The second suggestion I have is that the next time your husband does anything good, give him a verbal compliment. If he takes the garbage out, say "Dan, I want you to know that I really appreciate your taking the garbage out." . . . If you see him paying the electric bill, put your hand on his shoulder and say, "Dan, I really appreciate your paying the electric bill. I hear there are husbands who don't do that, and I want you to know how much I appreciate it." . . . Every time he does anything good, give him a verbal compliment.[67]

In the late twentieth century, readers consumed the idea that the job duties associated with being a successful wife still included a significant amount of performativity and husband-centered emotional labor, a kind of "intensive wifing" that mirrored the intensive mothering and child-centeredness popular during the same period.[68]

In the 2002 book *Wifework: What Marriage Really Means for Women*, the Australian journalist Susan Maushart offered a hard-hitting critique of precisely this "relentless routine of husband maintenance," wherein a heterosexually married man "does fewer chores, is happier, healthier and generally more satisfied," while a heterosexually married woman, "by contrast, will perform two to three times more unpaid physical, emotional, and organizational labor than her husband—and for a fraction of the rewards."[69] Maushart, writing in 2002, almost a century after William Robinson described the "indifference," "resentment," and "mutual ill-will" that characterized heterosexual marriage, painted a relatively unchanged portrait, one in which straight women deeply resent—but most often comply with—the pressure to reward their husbands for basic tasks like paying bills or taking out the trash. One of the great paradoxes of the heterosexual-repair industry is that this unreciprocated care of husbands is, at least according to Maushart, the reason that straight women initiate 75 percent of all divorces, but it is also relentlessly presented (albeit in ever-new forms of self-help) as the "solution" to women's misery. So great are the forces of patriarchy, misogyny, and the perceived costs associated with being an unaccommodating woman that slight variations on heterosexual misery are cast as preferable to feminist interventions.

By the end of twentieth century, straight couples learned that women and men are from two separate planets, with different languages, customs, and values. They learned that it is natural, or at least very common, for men to dislike spending substantial amounts of time in the company of their wives and that women should embrace rather than resist men's desire for spaces of freedom from marriage. Straight women learned that they, too, could seek freedom by maximizing their sexual capital and relying on women friends, just like the ladies of *Sex and the City*. Straight women learned that they should stop trying to change the men in their lives and should focus instead on finding ways to meet their own emotional needs. To the extent that women *do* need to ask something of men, they learned that they should do so with patient guidance and a hefty dose of gratitude.

## He's Just Not That into You

Moving into the twenty-first century, best-selling self-help books offered more nuanced and targeted messages about the link between marital success and women's willingness to provide men with exaggerated proclamations of gratitude and affirmation. For instance, Steve Harvey's number-one *New York Times* best-selling 2009 book *Act Like a Lady, Think Like a Man* sold over three million copies and was the first book of its kind to repackage many of the aforementioned ideas for Black women readers. Rehearsing a now predictable set of heterosexual-repair recommendations braided together with Black cultural references, Harvey counseled Black women to be at home when their men come home from work and to tell their husbands, "Baby, how was your day? Thank you for making it happen for us. This family needs you and wants you and is happy to have you." Evidence of the book's popularity among straight Black women can be found in the humorous confession of the feminist writer Brittney Cooper, who wrote in 2018, "I can ashamedly admit that I was one of the millions of Black women who made comedian Steve Harvey a best-selling author when I ran out and purchased his book. . . . Don't make me hand over my feminist card, please. A sister was desperate."[70] To the millions of Black women readers like Cooper, Harvey asserted, "We've got to feel like we're king, even if we don't act kingly. . . . A man needs that from his woman—he needs her to say, 'Baby, I can't tell you how much I appreciate what you do for me and the kids. . . . You so big and strong and you're everything that I need.' Those simple words give us the strength to keep on doing right by you and the family."[71] Notable in Harvey's book and its ilk is the continuation of a decades-old theme about men's emotional fragility and the tenuousness of heterosexual relationships. Men are depicted as needing a tremendous amount of praise, on par with what a mother might provide to a toddler to reinforce desired behaviors. But Harvey also delivered a more unsettling, though familiar, message by hinting that Black men are teetering on the verge of leaving (or ceasing to "do right by you and the family") if women do not provide this level of praise. Exemplifying the emotional labor expected of Black straight women and described by Michelle Wallace decades earlier, Harvey made clear that because Black men suffer the burden of anti-Black racism, it is in their homes and relationships that they must be treated like kings. Elided by all of this, of course, is Black women's own experience of anti-Black racism and the various ways it is compounded by the unique forms of misogyny that Black women endure, or what the queer Black feminist Moya Bailey has termed "misogynoir."[72]

Straight *women* self-help writers, drawing on their own experiences in the field of heterosexual dating, were more visible in the early 2000s, especially when their books possessed bold or sensational titles. One of these best sellers was Sherry Argov's 2002 book *Why Men Love Bitches: From Doormat to Dreamgirl—A Woman's Guide to Holding Her Own in a Relationship*. The book sold over one million copies, capturing the attention of straight women who, presumably, felt like doormats in relation to the men they had married or dated. The aim of *Why Men Love Bitches* was to help women readers elicit better treatment from men by teaching them to manipulate their husbands and boyfriends in order to earn their desire and loyalty. How would women do this? Here again, as if a new idea, Argov implored women to make sure their male partners always feel superior. Argov explained, "The three words guaranteed to turn any man on? 'You are right.' You'll never convince him otherwise, so don't bother trying. Let him be right. . . . Let a man think he's in control. When you appeal to his feelings of power, you charge up his batteries. Then you're giving him what he needs and he doesn't even know it."[73] A telling feature of the plucky "catch a man and keep him" books written by women in the early twenty-first century is that they advised women to relate to men in the most predictably sexist ways and yet framed this advice as a new form of empowerment or as an innovative set of weapons that a smart woman could use to manipulate men. In these texts, written as if centuries of patriarchy never occurred, women's submission to men was presented as a hot, new idea. For instance, at first glance, books such as Kara King's 2014 *The Power of the Pussy: How to Get What You Want from Men (Love, Respect, Commitment and More!)* would appear to take a fundamentally different approach from Laura Schlessinger's 2009 *The Proper Care and Feeding of Husbands*, the former centering women's needs and empowerment and the latter warn-

**Figure 2.4.** A scene from the 2012 film *Act Like a Lady, Think Like a Man*, based on Harvey's book.

ing women to focus on their husbands for the sake of their marriages. But both books followed in the same well-worn tradition of encouraging straight women to closely study men's psychology, suppress "female behaviors" that men "naturally" dislike (such as being too emotional), carefully tend to men's emotional needs, and manipulate men into a committed relationship.

In another ostensibly empowering twenty-first-century best seller, the 2004 book *He's Just Not That into You* (which inspired a movie by the same title), straight women were depicted as so desperate to partner with men that they would interpret any male behavior, including neglect or aggression, as a signal of love or interest. Harking back to Norwood's book thirty years earlier, coauthors Greg Behrendt and Liz Tuccillo dispelled women of this misconception, presenting them with the tough-love truth, "no, he's just not that into you." Seemingly a call to empower straight women, yet again, to walk away from disappointing men, the book's primary accomplishment was to revive early twentieth-century sexologists' popular dictum that "male desire is far less complicated" than women's.[74] Men don't have trust issues or trauma, they aren't grieving their last relationship, they are not too stressed-out with work to go on dates. The authors know this, they explained, because men are so motivated by sex that when they are sexually attracted to a woman, nothing else matters. If women think men are sending mixed messages, they are wrong; the truth is that men are just not sexually interested. Disguised as a form of pop-feminist self-help, *He's Just Not into You* reinforced the notion of a simple gender binary wherein straight women desperately grasp for men and straight men plod along with no logic, agency, or emotional depth whatsoever.

Thus far this chapter has focused on self-help books, by far the most popular and widely accessible forms of heterosexual repair. But it is worth noting that the heterosexual-repair industry takes many forms, several of which emerged or expanded in the late-capitalist period. The global sex- and romance-tourism industry, for instance, now targets both women and men, capitalizing on the broad range of reasons that straight people have become disillusioned with heterosexual courtship.[75] Homosocial online communities have also proliferated, offering spaces where straight men, in particular, can vent their frustrations with heterosexual relationships. One such community in the "manosphere," called Men Going Their Own Way, aims to empower antifeminist men to seek "sovereignty" from women by rejecting all heterosexual relationships in favor of forging bonds with men and occasionally paying for sex work.[76] Dating and relationship coaching is also a growing, international industry and the subject of chapter 3.

New Age self-actualization seminars and Christian megaevents are also popular spaces for heterosexual repair, merging long-standing bioessentialist arguments about gender difference—or masculine and feminine "energies" and "destinies"—with the project of personal transformation.[77] According to this arm of the heterosexual-repair industry, the secular world has promoted the false but politically correct idea that women and men are generally the same, a misconception that encourages people to deny their true essence and, consequently, wreaks havoc in heterosexual relationships. There is perhaps no better example of this approach than the seminars of the billionaire best-selling author, entrepreneur, business adviser, and motivational speaker Tony Robbins.[78] A 2016 Netflix documentary about Robbins's seminars, titled *I Am Not Your Guru*, directed by Joe Berlinger, reveals the role of heterosexual repair in the advice Robbins provides to the twenty-five hundred attendees at each of his "Date with Destiny" megaevents. Robbins teaches his followers that "feminine men" and "masculine women" are likely to be blocked in their ability to "discover their purpose" or "ignite their passion" because they are resisting their true essence or calling.

For instance, the documentary shows Robbins counseling a divorced woman named Hali, during which time he deduces that her father was too adoring when she was a child, resulting in her belief that she is entitled to men's love instead of needing to "work for it." When Hali explains that she is currently dating a man who is kind and gentle and loves to talk about his feelings, Robbins asserts that Hali has found herself another "feminine man" and pressures her to call him on the phone immediately and end the relationship. The film shows Hali breaking up with her boyfriend on the phone, for being too feminine, while the twenty-five hundred other "Date with Destiny" attendees look on, mesmerized by Robbins's power to change lives. In another intervention shown in the film, Robbins ascertains that an attendee named Lance also had a feminine father and that this made Lance too passive in his marriage to his wife, Tami. Robbins tells Lance the story of a lion cub raised by sheep who grows up believing he is a sheep, until the day an older male lion comes and kills his sheep family and forces him to eat their bodies. Robbins holds the microphone up to Lance, who, presumably inspired by this parable to recover his lost masculinity, belts out a lion's roar. Robbins yells, "Fuck yes, brother!!" and the event technicians bring up the "a dramatic breakthrough has occurred" music, the audience cheers and dances, and the camera pans to Tami, Lance's wife, who is smiling and clapping too. Later in the documentary, Tami and Lance report that they went back to their hotel room the night of the intervention, energized by the parable of the lion, had hot sex and decided to have children.

Robbins's seminars are a stunning example of the cyclical nature of the tragedy of heterosexuality; the very gender binarism and misogyny that produce heterosexual misery are also the interventions proffered to consumers to remedy it. Robbins's personal coaching also exemplifies the self-improvement focus of twenty-first-century heterosexual repair, in that it reframes men's power over women not only as a winning relationship strategy but also as an act of spiritual wholeness that brings out the best in men and women, aligning them with their "path."[79]

## The Long Campaign

Among the many expert discourses that emerged in the twentieth century to give form to the new "heterosexual" and her/his desire for the opposite sex, one message was consistently clear: heterosexuality was a difficult accomplishment, a hard sell, a campaign in need of propaganda, and a white-supremacist project. For early sexologists, heterosexual marriage was synonymous with sexual violence and visceral repulsion. If heterosexual identity were to succeed as the model for normal, healthy sexuality in the modern era, men's violence and misogyny would need tempering. The emergence of "normal heterosexuality" also relied on and bolstered anti-Black racism by positioning the benevolent patriarchy of white marriages as the standard against which African American sexuality would be evaluated. Later, for midcentury psychologists, marriage amounted to a tenuous merging of unequals, its success wholly dependent on the selflessness, and emotional and domestic labor, of white and Black women devoted to men's public and private pursuits. In the 1980s and '90s, alarmed psychologists pointed out that millions of straight men still hated women and that marriages were the battleground where the war of the sexes was being waged. By the late twentieth and early twenty-first centuries, experts warned that men had grown tired of women's demands for autonomy, or tired of feminism, and were craving women's gratitude—yet again. By the late twentieth century, Black writers like Steve Harvey had adopted the same heteropatriarchal rhetoric canonized by white male self-help writers in previous decades, advising straight Black women that submission and gratitude were the key to Black men's loyalty.

Our tour through the heterosexual-repair industry has also pointed to a significant shift in the patriarchal contract. Under classic white-supremacist heteropatriarchy, men extracted women's reproductive and emotional labor in exchange for the promise of economic and physical protection—a promise often unkept given the violence that husbands themselves committed against their wives. Married heterosexual women also received some symbolic forms of power and respect in exchange for their submission, providing them with greater status in the hierarchy of women. But as early feminist critiques of this exchange gained traction in the nineteenth and twentieth centuries, so too did sexologists and psychologists increase their investments in, and expectations of, heterosexuality. Men were now urged to provide love and friendship in exchange for women's subservience and deep gratitude. Men and women would now aspire to like each other, even if this required tremendous compromise, complaint, and feigned interest.

By the mid-twentieth century, as modern capitalism shored up the links between American masculinity, rationality, and individualism—making it no longer as viable for men to be romantically connected to one another—it was with women, and within the private heterosexual family, that men's fragility could be expressed. Women, already degraded, became the figures who could witness men's fragility, especially given that fragility itself was cast as a degraded and feminized state of being. But this, too, produced backlash, an amplification of the fear that loving women too much, or being too dependent on their care and attention, would threaten men's power.

I hope this chapter has also illuminated the ways that straight women have struggled with and against the tragedy of heterosexuality, not only by consuming self-help strategies they hoped would improve their lives but also by tirelessly calling out misogyny and its effects on their re-lationships. As I write this book, the song "Truth Hurts" by the Black feminist rapper Lizzo has topped the popular-music charts. Lizzo sings, "Yeah, I got boy problems. That's the human in me. Bling bling, then I solve 'em. That's the goddess in me. . . . You're 'posed to hold me down, but you're holding me back, And that's the sound of me not calling you back" (incidentally, Lizzo wrote the song with three male songwriters, two white men and one Asian man). Countless videos on Instagram show girls and women belting out these lyrics at Lizzo concerts. Like generations of straight feminist women before them, they are celebrat-ing the possibility that women could just say no to bad men; they could be goddesses, filled with self-love, who just don't call those men back. But the history, or rather the herstory, of heterosexual repair suggests that, ultimately, straight women still experience desire and/or pressure to find a male partner and get married, and with this desire/pressure the opportunities for feminist resistance begin to narrow, the walls of het-eronormativity close in, and straight women find themselves in the self-help aisle of the bookstore, reading *Act Like a Lady, Think Like a Man*.

# 3

# PICKUP ARTISTS

## Inside the Seduction Industry

$I$ AM AT A BOUTIQUE HOTEL ON THE FAMED SUNSET STRIP in West Hollywood. I wait outside the locked conference-room door, the first to arrive. Soon a couple of men shuffle out of the elevator, surveying the foyer sheepishly. I overhear one ask the other, "Are you here for the Bible study?" They both laugh, the joke an ice-breaking acknowledgment that perhaps the real seminar they are about to attend, the one that will teach them the secrets of how to seduce young hot women, should be kept incognito.[1]

After watching the online advertising trailers for the Love Systems Bootcamp that we are about to enter, I am expecting a large banquet hall full of men. I have learned from these promo videos that the Love Systems Annual Super Conference in Las Vegas draws hundreds of men seeking to learn how to "generate women's attraction" and become informed of the "newest / most powerful breakthroughs in dating science." But today, at this regional bootcamp in West Hollywood, I have been granted access to observe a much smaller and more intimate Love Systems event. Ten men eventually filter into the small, sunlit conference room, seated around an oval seminar table. I, the researcher, and the only woman present, sit in the corner of the room. When invited to introduce myself, I explain to the bootcamp participants that I am a sociologist from UC Riverside, writing a book that will include a chapter on the seduction industry and "what it might tell us about the state of contemporary gender relations." I promise them confidentiality and explain that while I am taking notes, I will not record their names or other identifying information about them. But they are palpably uninterested in my short, obligatory speech. They have no questions for me. They are ready to get started, to begin this two-day seminar "guaranteed to teach men how to get out of the 'friend zone' and pick up beautiful women." And, in case you are wondering, I find out fairly quickly that I am not one of the women they are interested in seducing. A thirty-eight-year-old feminist, I am far too old, too serious. Perfect. I am just a fly on the wall.

* * *

In recent years, many of the self-help messages that were once directed primarily at straight women have been extended to straight men. In the new twenty-first-century self-help paradigm, men, too, have been wronged by modern heterosexuality. As the experts explain, this is because women now control the terms of seduction and sex, leaving men feeling powerless and resentful. Men consumers of today's heterosexual-repair services learn that their desperation, insecurity, and aggression are off-putting to women; that their bodies might be undesirable—too short, too bald, too old, or too fat to compete with other men; that women experience their flirtation tactics as creepy and awkward, if not threatening and scary; and that men need the help of trained professionals to overcome these deficiencies. In other words, straight men are finally burdened with some of the labor of making heterosexual desire functional, though they come to this work, as did their early twentieth-century counterparts who resisted loving women, with fear and ambivalence.

One realm where men have turned for help is the dating and seduction industry, in which "seduction coaches" train men to relearn the basics of heterosexual attraction in a post-#metoo era. Many of these coaching businesses evolved out of the controversial and misogynistic "pickup artist" subculture of the early 2000s but have since rebranded their services as a more holistic and feminist-friendly approach to men's self-actualization. Dating coaches offer a broad array of psychotherapeutic, informational, and strategic interventions into men's troubled relationships with women. They help straight men heal the anxiety and depression caused by women's sexual rejection. They normalize men's sexual failures by explaining the evolutionary and sociocultural causes of sexual rejection using what they call "dating science." And they teach men to perform new expressions of heteromasculinity aimed at making straight women feel safe and understood.

The strategies used by dating and seduction coaches are composed of old, new, and repurposed attempts to reconcile heterosexual desire with misogyny; intimacy with "faking"; feminism with the science of gender difference; and seemingly private problems with neoliberal interventions (self-actualization seminars, personal coaching, and other financial investments in personal and relational improvement). Their industry is also a transnational and imperialist one; as American and European coaches offer seduction bootcamps around the globe, they name and then "solve" the heterosexual disappointments and desires of men in the global South. To illuminate these complex dynamics, this chapter draws on field notes from two weekend-long seduction bootcamps I attended in 2013–2014, interviews with seduction coaches, weekly newsletters subscriptions about how to seduce women, and over fifty videos and webinar clips from seduction bootcamps and in-field trainings. In 2013, the year I began my investigation of dating and seduction coaching, I obtained access to two well-established and high-profile seduction-coaching companies: Love Systems, a company based in Los Angeles and owned by a coach with ties to the original pickup-artist scene; and the Noble Art of Seduction, a woman-owned London-based company that regularly offered classes in Los Angeles.[2] Later, in 2017, I shifted focus to a newer training program, Project Rockstar, an immersive offshoot of Love Systems that offers men "a complete life transformation."

## Pickup Artists: The Roots of the Seduction Industry

Seduction or dating coaching companies emerged in the early 2000s as the purportedly more respectable, corporate arm of what had been called the "pickup artist" community—a subculture that elicited widespread controversy following the 2005 publication of Neil Strauss's notorious book *The Game*. Part ethnography, part how-to guide, Strauss's book chronicled the journalist's entrée into an international secret society of schlubby straight white men who claimed to have cracked the code for getting "hot" women around the globe to have "same night" sex with them. *The Game* was a global best seller, and pickup artistry subsequently expanded into a high-profile international industry in which expert coaches—usually, but not always, men—offered weekend boot-camps in which they taught other men "game," or how to seduce women, for a fee ranging from $1,500 to $4,000. Many of these expert coaches were not conventionally attractive men. In fact, in the early development of the industry, the more average the man (the balder, the older, the chubbier, the less wealthy, the more effeminate), the more impressive were his credentials as a seducer of young, attractive women. This is because a key selling point of pickup-artist seminars was their embrace of the AFC, or average frustrated chump. The frustrated chump took many forms: the social outcast who stayed a virgin longer than his friends, the introverted guy who was afraid to approach women and felt stuck in "the friend zone," the immigrant man who hadn't mastered American gender norms or was still learning how to flirt in English, the involuntarily gay-acting straight guy, the socially awkward computer programmer—and the list of frustrated men went on and on.

Seduction coaches promised to alleviate these men's sexual suffering by teaching them what kind of masculinity to embrace, and what kind to avoid, in the service of attracting women. They warned men that the flip side of being a seemingly harmless chump was appearing to be a creepy dude, a man whose desperation makes him appear lecherous and unsafe to the very women he is trying to impress. At pickup-artist trainings, coaches welcomed these often depressed, vulnerable, and unintentionally creepy men without judgment, assuring them that the power to seduce women is not innate but simply a learned set of skills. During interviews, coaches told me that most men believe that attracting women should come naturally, so they enter trainings with a deep sense of personal deficiency and, in some cases, self-loathing. To resolve this, coaches told trainees that other men who appear to be "naturals" at seduction were most likely taught by their fathers and brothers how to approach women. For men who did not receive this early guidance, coaches were proxy mentors, brotherly or fatherly figures, who could help bring them up to speed. The coaches also offered lengthy testimony about their own sexless lives before discovering the game; the more tragic their stories of failure with women, the more powerfully the stories functioned as evidence that attraction is an acquired skill available to all men willing to invest the time and money to achieve it. These "former losers," now financially successful seduction coaches, explained that they have now had sex with hundreds of hot women, or they have five women fuckbuddies on speed-dial, or they have a gorgeous girlfriend, and so on—compelling credentials coming from these bald, dorky, or otherwise unexpected Casanovas.

A stunning example of the misogyny paradox, pickup artists built their success on helping other men resolve the tension between straight men's socialization, on the one hand, and straight women's reality, on the other. They spoke directly to men's sense of a lost heterosexual birthright and an unfulfilled media-fueled expectation that men, no matter how average in personality or appearance, would have access to a reasonable amount of uncomplicated sex with women they find attractive.[3] The filmmaker Sut Jhally calls this the "male dreamworld," a fantasy world in which young, beautiful women are presented to boys and men as an entitlement,[4] and the feminist writer Laura Kipnis, too, has noted the perplexing disparity between powerful, straight, white men's inflated sense of their own appeal and their over-the-top requirements of the women they desire (Kipnis describes men like Harvey Weinstein and Donald Trump as "bulbous, jowly men; fat men who told women they needed to lose weight; ugly men drawn to industries organized around female appearance").[5] But as pickup artists knew, many men reached the pinnacle of heterosexual misery when their dreamworld could no long integrate real women. In reality, the women these men encountered had grown tired of men's sense of entitlement, their scripted flirtations, their braggadocio, and their aggressive and self-centered approach to sex.

**Figure 3.1.** A session at the annual Love Systems Super Conference in Las Vegas. (From Love Systems website)

The Love Systems Bootcamp was the first seduction training I attended, and Love Systems is still in business in 2019 as I write this book. Nick Savoy, its owner, had been involved in the early and notorious iterations of pickup culture described by Neil Strauss, but he had since disavowed the term "pickup artist" and self-identified as a "dating coach" whose work was based on "relationship science." As I described at the start of this chapter, I spent the weekend in the small hotel seminar room with Savoy, two other male Love Systems trainers, a handful of their male assistants, and the ten men students who had registered in the course. Notwithstanding the fact that these men generously gave me permission to observe the seminar, I expected to hate them. But, as other scholars and journalists who have entered the seduction industry have noted,[6] one of the immediately observable features of the trainings is the likability of many of the men who circulate within them, a feeling that stems largely from their vulnerability and mutual care once inside the protected space of the seminar. I described this mood in my field notes:

> I am really struck by their friendliness with each other, their kindness, the absence of posturing that I am accustomed to in male-dominated faculty meetings! The mood is like one part friendly slumber party, one part physical therapy—with trainers teaching the men to breathe from

the chest, to be more natural in their posture and movement, and to use proper skincare products. They recommended a specific glycolic exfoliant to use after shaving and the best height-increasing shoes for shorter men! The intimacy of this part of the training feels sweet to me. During breakout dyads, the trainer showed one of the men how to gently touch a woman's hair at a bar.

Some of the men's faces flushed when it was their turn to speak, or their voices trembled when they talked about problems they've had with women. I feel sorry for them. The feeling is a lot like group therapy. It seems like . . . the mood of an infertility group for women? These men thought they were entitled to something (hot chicks!), but it isn't happening. They are confused about why it isn't happening.

During introductions, each participant explained his reasons for being there: "I want to work on approaching women and having fewer dry spells"; "I am forty-three and play volleyball, and I do meet girls doing that. But I need the skills to close the deal"; "I feel awkward, and like I'm not very interesting. I don't have much experience with women"; "I travel the world and have been with a lot of women, but I want hotter women. I want more high-quality pussy!"; "I get tired after work, so I just don't have the motivation to go out"; "I can talk to girls, but it never ends up being sexual. I end up being the friend guy." Two European men mentioned that they had success with women outside of the United States but found American women to be unapproachable. Several men mentioned that they wanted the ability be more selective, to have sex with women who were more attractive than the ones who seemed interested in them. One of the trainers quickly affirmed that this is a common theme for men: "Men want to be able to choose, not settle for the low-hanging fruit. We're going to make that happen." My sympathy for some of these men—men heartbroken by the low-hanging fruit—started to wane.

During a break, with my best tone of nonjudgmental, ethnographic geniality, I approached the British man in his fifties who had expressed his desire for more "high-quality pussy" and asked him what, precisely, he meant by that. As soon as the words came out of my mouth, he turned bright red and said, "Oh, now I am *mortified* you are asking me that! I should not have said that! You must think I am terrible." I told him I genuinely wanted to understand what the comment meant. Was it literally about the quality of women's vaginas? I asked, playing naïve. Was it about a certain type of woman? What did "quality" mean? He said, "Yeah, it's about the whole package. I would like to find a beautiful woman who has a lot of energy for fun and adventure. That's all I meant, actually." Over the course of both bootcamps I attended, older men commonly named "fun" and "adventurousness" as among women's most desirable traits. The more they shared about the kind of women they did *not* want (divorced women, serious women, jaded women, women focused on parenting their children), the more it became clear that "fun" and "adventurous" were codes men used to describe women much younger than themselves.

At the second bootcamp I attended in 2013, this one offered by the London-based company Noble Art of Seduction, a male seduction coach conducted an exercise designed to reduce men's anxiety around young, beautiful women by helping trainees knock these women off their symbolic pedestals. The coach painted an image for the male trainees of a tall, thin, beautiful blond in her early twenties and then asked the men to visualize the reality of her life. He said, "She makes minimum wage at Forever 21, she's sharing a small apartment with her friend, she's just beginning to understand how the world works, and if she's like most girls, she's probably insecure about her body."[7] The coach then explained to the men that *they* have the power. They have more life experience, they probably have more money, and if they develop their game, they will exude a competent masculinity to which these insecure young women will be drawn. When two men in their early forties expressed that they felt afraid to approach women in their twenties, the coach responded, "[Your age] is your advantage. Think back to high school: girls dated guys in higher grades. Women want to date older men." Kezia Noble, a woman and the company's owner and lead coach, concurred, warning an older student never to answer a younger woman's question about how old he is by saying, "Can you guess?" "Older men like to say that all the time, but you should *never* say that. You are a grown man," Noble told him. "Tell her your age right away. You have *lived*. You're experienced, more mature. You have inner confidence. Your age is an advantage. Use it. If she asks, 'How old are you?' you say, 'Old enough to be your father. And it's past your bedtime!'"

Kezia Noble's seduction students included a mix of African American, Latino, white, and non-American men, both white and of color. Over and over again, male students across a range of socioeconomic and racial/ethnic backgrounds expressed desire for the most well-worn, predictable, and arguably retro fantasy of an attractive woman: young, thin, white, and blond.[8] Despite being surrounded at the time by popular, booty-centric images of Jennifer Lopez, Kim Kardashian, and other women who had risen to fame, at least in part, on the power of their curves (a departure from the blond, thin women in fashion in the 1980s and '90s, the Christie Brinkleys and Elle MacPhersons who appeared on posters in boys' bedrooms and mechanics' shops around the country), white-supremacist hierarchies of beauty ensured that the figure of the skinny blonde still held sway over these men. When Chris, a twenty-five-year-old African American man from Chicago was asked by a coach to describe his ideal woman in more detail, he replied, "She needs to believe in God, be down-to-earth, white, blond, and shorter than me." Demonstrating for trainees how to visualize in detail one's ideal type beyond generic descriptions like "hot" or "nice," a white male coach called forth the image of his own ne plus ultra of sexy girls, "I love girls who are skinny and blond with really good posture, like dancers. You know those girls who have a curve in their back, from such great posture? Full lips, high cheekbones, makeup that highlights her eyes, not big breasts. I know it's tough to be specific, because it's the first time you have sat down to think about something other than blond and big breasts. But we're doing this so we won't settle out of convenience."

**Figure 3.2.** Kezia Noble's bootcamp. (From www.Kezia-Noble.com)

Sprinkled throughout these bootcamps were also numerous confidence-building, self-improvement platitudes about how men need to be willing to fail, trust the journey, have an abundance mind-set, know that it takes time to build skills, and so on. Coaches also gave extensive attention to what they called "inner game" by replacing men's defeatist psychology with a willingness to get "blown out," or rejected by numerous women, without being psychologically annihilated by it. Seduction trainees were taught that the best mind-set for seducing women is not to be attached to any particular woman but to approach enough beautiful women to get rejected dozens of times, until men move into a relaxed, abundance-oriented, nothing-to-lose frame of mind. This "fail harder" ethos comes directly from corporate, sales-driven motivational frameworks, which, as the sociologist Rachel O'Neill argues in her outstanding study of London-based seduction bootcamps, makes seduction less of a game than it is a form of work, in which men become sexual entrepreneurs who approach sex in terms of long-term investment and increased returns.[9] Bootcamps are also places where men learn "best practices," or proven seduction routines, which they practice together during their group sessions and also out at bars and clubs during "infield training." Male trainees are given the opportunity, during infield training, to try their approach on dozens of women, while their supportive coaches and fellow trainees are waiting in the wings to debrief what did and did not work and to encourage men to quickly move on to the next approach.

Trainees also learn the basic anatomy of seduction, with coaches offering examples of how to complete each step in the seduction process: the initial approach, transitioning into conversation, attracting her (showing her your value and building her interest), qualifying her (playfully getting her to show interest in you, determining whether it's worthwhile to continue the seduction), comforting her (offering some brief moments of an authentic get-to-know-you connection), and finally, seduction (touching her, making sexual comments, making clear that sex is your intention). Love Systems trainers explained that one commonly used tactic to qualify women, or build their interest, is to "neg" them, but that this "old-school tactic" is now considered needlessly antagonistic.[10] To neg a woman is to make subtly critical or teasing comments about her to show a lack of interest and trigger her insecurity, thereby leveling the playing field (such as, "I wish you were a brunette. I'm taking a break from blondes for a while," or "Eww, you just spit on me!" or "Hey, just cause I'm Asian, you're not going to talk to me?"). According to the coaches at Love Systems, although the negging technique has a bad reputation, some mild and playful negs, used sparingly, are proven to work because they do the opposite of what women expect. Instead of fawning over women and showering them with false compliments, men can neg women to show that they are confident enough not to beg for attention.

## The Misogyny Paradox, Revisited

In 2014, it became clear that pickup-artist subculture was inspiring real-life violence against women. First was Elliot Rodger, the twenty-two-year-old male student who killed seven people in Isla Vista, California, because, by his own admission, he wanted revenge on the women who did not find him attractive. Rodger was a follower of pickup-artist websites and used the lingo of the subculture in his suicide video. Later that year, the horrific misogyny and racism of Julien Blanc, the owner of a popular pickup-artist company called Real Social Dynamics, caused international outrage. Blanc had posted a video to YouTube in which he can be seen in Tokyo, grabbing Japanese women on the street and in bars and pushing their heads toward his penis. In captured video footage of his seminar, he was seen telling attendees, "If you're a white male, you can do what you want. I'm just romping through the streets, just grabbing girls' heads, just like, head, *pfft* [sound effect] on the dick." His Instagram profile also showed photos of him with his hands around women's throats, with the hashtag #chokinggirlsaroundtheworld. A few years later, in 2018, Alek Minassian killed ten people in Toronto after posting on Facebook that Elliot Rodger was his inspiration to kick-start the "Incel Rebellion," or the murderous revenge plot of "involuntarily celibate" men.[11] As the media exposed these cases as examples of the violence of the seduction industry, numerous commentators offered their analyses of the seduction curriculum and its peddlers. *Psychology Today* described the game as a set of "quasi-psychological tricks" used to prey on and exploit women;[12] *The Guardian* described the game as "sinister" and "pathetic," run by "alienated and dysfunctional" men intoxicated by other men's approval even more than heterosexual sex itself;[13] *Vice* called the game a "set of personal, tailored approaches and carefully-crafted individualized steps for bamboozling women;"[14] *Jezebel* echoed these analyses, describing pickup artists as predators who believe that women "can be 'understood' via dangerous, antiquated notions of femininity and conquered using emotional and physical manipulation," with seemingly no limit to how far men will go to exert sexual control.[15]

But some of these critiques also had the effect of obscuring the fact that much of the seduction industry looks less like these extreme expressions of hypermisogyny and more like a perfectly predictable outgrowth of the heterosexual-repair industry, or the run-of-the-mill misogyny that has troubled modern heterosexual relationships from the start. Most seduction coaches and pickup artists base their work on the same premise that was phenomenally popular when John Gray circulated it in the 1990s with *Men Are from Mars, Women Are from Venus* and when Steve Harvey circulated it in *Act Like a Lady, Think Like a Man* in 2009: namely, that men and women want fundamentally different things out of heterosexuality, and as a result, their attraction and relationships are fraught with conflict and misunderstanding. Seduction coaches, at some level, know that heterosexuality's continued fragility and failure produce a demand for interventions that can build women's sexual desire for average men and increase average men's capacity to elicit that desire. So while commentators critiqued the pickup-artist industry for teaching men to be "fake" with women in order to have sex with them, this kind of performativity was certainly nothing new; as self-help writers have told the millions of straight people who have bought their books, heterosexuality works best when men and women learn to say and do things that they don't actually want to say or do, for the sake of heterosexuality—to express interest, gratitude, and connection, whether they feel it or not. In the heterosexual-repair industry, this is not about manipulation; it is about learning an advanced relationship skill.

Some journalists, observing that the seduction industry seemed to be addressing problems endemic to heterosexuality, offered more equivocal accounts of the seduction curriculum by noting its emphasis on fostering confidence and emotional intelligence in anxious men who had been made emotionally deficient—awkward, creepy, and otherwise unappealing—by male gender socialization. Quoted in *Jezebel*, a woman and self-identified "feminist pickup artist" insisted that good seduction trainers "are devoted to fostering intimacy, not creepy coercion."[16] A journalist for *Vice* declared, "Everyone thinks the 'trained' pickup artist is a sleazy, predatory lizard [who is] stalking women. The truth is some are like that, but quite a lot of them, I can tell you, are painfully shy guys who break out in sweats at the thought of even speaking to a girl."[17] And a *Jezebel* blogger who described many seduction techniques as "sinister" also confessed that much of what she saw while working as an employee for a seduction company did not offend her: "the advice was based on building men up, as opposed to denigrating women."[18]

This equivocation about the meaning and effects of seduction coaching mirrors some of the ambivalence I too had felt while immersed inside the bootcamps. For one thing, no one likes the idea that sexuality is scripted and formulaic, even when it is. The idea that heterosexual seduction can be reduced to such a predictable formula and that young, straight women can be taken in by more or less clever pickup lines is an affront to a centuries-long heteropatriarchal campaign about the unique and mystical nature of romance itself (a campaign that has long served as an ideological cover for women's oppression at the hands of men who claimed to love them). But, on the other hand, the seduction industry also makes a kind of logical and familiar sense within the culture and political economy of the twenty-first century. It not only builds on a century of popular and scientific theorizing about purportedly natural gender differences and the trouble they cause well-intentioned straight people, but it also upholds the value of individual self-actualization (i.e., taking dramatic steps to know yourself and get what you want, right now) and embraces neoliberal mantras once reserved for corporate motivational posters, applying them to heterosexual sex ("Fail harder!" "Embrace a mastery mind-set!" "Show her your leadership!"). As Rachel O'Neill contends, "The [seduction] industry borrows from and is informed by many of the same knowledge formations that undergird heterosexual sex and relationship advice more generally, most particularly that of evolutionary psychology, a major purveyor of 'two sexes, two cultures' paradigm."[19] Hence, for me the question was not whether I "agreed" with the seduction coaches or thought they were approaching heterosexuality in the most ethical, feminist way possible (that answer would obviously be no) but whether their approach made enough sense in the current cultural moment to perhaps actually *work* on straight women and, dare I say, perhaps even be an improvement on what straight men were doing before they learned to reflect on the difference between creeps and noncreeps.

Because misogyny has so profoundly overdetermined the ways that most straight men approach women in bars and other sexualized settings, many seduction coaches could fairly easily predict what it would take for a given man to set himself apart from the legions of creepy dudes, sexually aggressive men, and arrogant mansplainers. Their aim was not an altruistic or feminist one; in the end, I did not believe they were motivated by a desire to make straight men less creepy for its own sake. Instead, they observed that women don't like creeps and that men can get what they want (sex) if they give women what women want (connection, humble confidence, basic decency). Closely mirroring the presumptions of twentieth-century sexologists and psychologists, seduction coaches worked from the premise that most men, in their natural state, are not what straight women want. And most women, in their natural state, are not what men want (if "natural" includes over thirty-five, average-looking, divorced, fat, of color, mothers, etc.). Their work illuminates that straight culture exists in a very conflicted relationship to what I have elsewhere called "gender labor,"[20] the intimate work that must be done to make both heterosexual attraction and the gender binary appear natural. On the one hand, gender labor smooths out the contradictions, but on the other hand, the very act of doing this labor exposes heterosexuality as a high-maintenance, nonautomatic project.

## Building Empathy and Safety: Seduction Strategies That (Might) Work

What *does* it take for a straight man to set himself apart from the creeps and earn a woman's trust and desire? As Kezia Noble, the owner of Noble Art of Seduction, explained to the men attending her bootcamp, men must first understand the reasons that women refuse eye contact, shut down conversation, and otherwise reject men who approach them in public places. Noble does not use the phrase "rape culture" in her seminar, though she arguably describes it. She encourages trainees to view the world through women's eyes by imagining what it must be like to be endlessly and aggressively approached by men trying to coerce women into sex. Men boast, lie, and play power games with women, she explains. Women have seen it all and are exhausted. So when a "good man" looking for a fun time approaches an attractive woman, of course she is going to put up her "bitch shield" or give him a "shit test," Noble proclaims. In the seduction community, bitch shields (i.e., being rude to, or ignoring, men) and shit tests (i.e., insulting men) are recognized as survival strategies women have developed to manage sexual objectification. Both Kezia's team of coaches and the coaches from Love Systems explained to the men in their seminars that when women ignore or dismiss them in social environments, it is not because they are actually bitches but because they have put up a shield that is necessary to manage the overwhelming sexual attention they receive from aggressive and/or frightening men. Trainees learned to understand that the "AFOG," or the alpha female of the group—the woman who protects her women friends from aggressive men in bars—is also a necessary figure in women's social worlds, another component of women's survival strategy.

A male coach working on Noble's team asked bootcamp participants to put themselves in women's shoes by also considering the slut shaming that prevents straight women from expressing desire in the same ways encouraged of men: "If a man sleeps around, he's celebrated. But there's a double standard, and women are called sluts. It's ridiculous, but that's what women have got to deal with. So if she makes eye contact, that's her version of an approach. That's all she can do." Later he told trainees to be highly attentive to women's sense of safety: "Keep an arm's reach apart. . . . Fix yourself on a wall or pole, so she feels safe. She has the option to leave. Find something to lean on, so you don't look like a threat. As a rule, [say your opening line] and take one step back! Give her room, a safe talking distance so she feels comfortable."

Rather than resent women's strategies for negotiating men's sexual aggression, trainees were told to recognize and *work with* them.

Coaches encouraged them to make self-deprecating jokes, to bond with women about how creepy other men are, to befriend the AFOG, and sometimes even to play-act at being gay in order to put women initially at ease. All of these strategies at first seemed ridiculously counterintuitive to the seduction students. They thought that in those few precious moments after approaching a woman, they were supposed to sell themselves by referencing how much money they had or showing off some other form of power that would give them a competitive edge over other men. But they gradually came to understand the social context—the context of rape culture and male aggression—in which self-deprecating humor and other displays of vulnerability, including sexual, gendered, socioeconomic, and racial vulnerability, make sense. Love Systems coaches gave the following examples of jokes that trainees could try:

- "What? I was totally going to wear that [*point to her outfit*]. Oh how embarrassing!"
- "My mom sent me here to lose my virginity. Do you think I have a shot?" [The coach explains that "anything about being a virgin, having a small penis, being gay, being dropped off by your mom—ironically, these all get a laugh and really make women comfortable."]
- Be goofy and wrong on purpose: "If the woman you're approaching is Black, you say, 'So what part of Korea are you from? North? South?'"
- Point to a creepy or drunk dude and say, "Oh, your dad is really out of control tonight. You shouldn't have brought him."
- For men of color seducing white women, say, "You think because you're white, you are better than me? Oh, so you're a racist!"
- "I really like you, so it's too bad I am broke. Yeah, I sleep in a dumpster close to here. It's convenient though!"

Coaches explained that role reversals, wherein men pretend to be worried about their own safety or offended by women's objectification of them, can also be humorous and subtle ways of acknowledging the importance of safety, thereby putting women at ease, especially in club or bar environments. They offered these suggestions:

- Point to her, and then turn to her friend and ask, "She's gorgeous, but can I trust her? Is she safe?"
- Say loudly, "No I will *not* make out with you!" or "No I will *not* show you my penis in public!"
- Say, "Just so you know, it's boys' night tonight. We're just here to dance together, so don't try anything."
- If she says, "You're funny. I like you," you can say, "Whoa! Whoa! Don't get any ideas!"

Lines like these cast men as willing victims of women's sexual lecherousness, and as cheesy and absurd as they may seem and as much as they may risk making light of women's actual experiences of unwanted sexual attention, coaches explained that they temporarily shift the objectifying gaze to men's bodies, giving straight women a reprieve and inviting them—should they be interested—to inhabit the role of sexual aggressor. While many critics of the seduction industry have dismissed its curriculum as a set of garden-variety pickup lines that most women would "see right through," coaches are emphatic that their routines are effective precisely because they shake up the tired terrain of heterosexual flirtation by teaching trainees to do the opposite of what most men do when they are attracted to women.

During an interview with Ben, a Love Systems trainer, I shared my surprise at how much of the seduction curriculum was focused on figuring out the best ways not to be "creepy"—exactly the opposite of what most commentators had imagined was happening in these men-only seminars on how to pick up women. Ben smiled and responded, "People are suspicious about this work at first. They have an impression of who would do this, these creepy guys. I was worried about being part of it myself. But really it's not about that. . . . We are teaching guys who aren't naturals how to interact with women. One of the trainers tells his mom all about what he does, and she's proud of him! She says he is saving the world from boring and creepy guys, one guy at a time." Ben's framing of the seduction industry as a gift, rather than a threat, to women was echoed by other coaches I spoke with, both men and women, who seemed to genuinely believe that they were helping to repair heterosexuality by aligning straight men's behavior with what women actually want. As Kezia Noble instructed her trainees on how to be less boring and weird, she offered them the following insight:

> Some pickup artists will suggest you ask a kooky question, like, "I'm going to a costume party. Should I go as James Bond or Fred Flintstone?" That's *weird*. Let's talk about the normal questions that come up. She asks, "What do you do [for a living]." You tell her the truth. . . . Most of you are doing a job that you wouldn't do for free, that you don't actually love. If she asks, "Do you like your job?" and you don't, you show your passion: "This job I'm doing is not all that, but I'm making a lot of money, and I get to do these other things I love with that money." This [kind of answer] is real. She will be attracted to your passion. What you need to convey is that you love your *life*. You can even say, "I fucking hate my job, but I love my life." Even hating something is passion. It's the opposite of boring.

In the sociologist Diana Scully's study of seventy-nine convicted rapists, she makes the compelling argument that men rape women when they lack the ability to "role-take," or to see themselves from women's perspective and feel the role-taking emotions—guilt, shame, and empathy—that produce self-control.[21] Her work implies that the ubiquity of rape should come as no surprise, given what limited training boys and men have in how to identify with girls and women or to reflect on what the world is like from women's point of view. In many ways, a significant portion of the seduction curriculum I encountered was aimed at asking men to "role-take" in exactly the way Scully describes—to consider how women are experiencing heterosexual flirtation. On the surface of things, clients of seduction companies are purchasing an increased chance at having sex with women; but more substantively, in the seminars themselves, what men receive in return for their enrollment fee is an entire weekend reflecting on what women actually want from men and from heterosexual sex itself.

Witnessing this curriculum unfold, I felt a good amount of anger and repulsion at the way so many straight men were still, after decades of feminist and antiracist interventions, obsessed with young white girls (seduction coaches commonly use the term "girl" to refer to women of all ages). But I also felt cautiously optimistic in moments as I watched these men struggle to understand sex through women's eyes, an ability I had long believed, since reading Scully's work years ago, to be a key ingredient in the undoing of rape culture. I am under no illusion that seduction training prevents men from raping, in part because these trainings rarely spend much time attending to what actually happens once trainees and the women they have seduced transition from public to private space, where sex is believed by many men to be a foregone conclusion. But the curriculum does ask men to actively disavow aggressive masculinity, to exercise empathy, and to spend more time than they've ever spent thinking about the rigged conditions under which straight women must negotiate sex with men.

## Masculinity and Sexual Leadership

One of the fundamental premises of the seduction industry is that men and women are hardwired differently and that, for bioevolutionary reasons, straight women are attracted to men's sexual leadership. Male trainees learn that women want to be brought into a man's fun and already-complete world; they want men to "curate" the experiences they have together. As one Love Systems coach explained, "You as the man have to *lead*, and she has to come into *your* world. Don't put pressure on her to lead because she does not want to. She doesn't want to take responsibility for that. She wants you to be the rock, the one creating the energy, and she is going to oscillate around it. You put masculine energy out there, and girls follow it. This way you are giving value. You are not taking something from her but offering something to her. You are already having fun, and she wants to join in." At the Noble Art of Seduction bootcamp, a coach made a very similar speech: "You are a man, and she wants you to lead. If you've already determined that you aren't worthy of her, that she's out of your league, then you have already failed her. It's not that complicated: women just want you to show up as a man." The same coach later proclaimed that trainees must never second-guess the appropriateness of approaching women or doubt that women want them to take charge of sex and romance: "Women will say that *they* want to lead, but they don't. They watch all these romantic comedies. They want the fantasy, the fairy tale. All women want this. The woman who met her partner because he came flying in out of nowhere while she was getting coffee is the woman with the romantic story that all her friends envy." And because no discussion of male sexual leadership would be complete without a war metaphor, a coach described it this way: "She may tell you not to go off to war, but if you don't, you won't be a man and now . . . she won't respect you. It's the same in a club."

Love Systems promotional materials promise the men who attend their bootcamps and conferences that they will learn "the biggest breakthroughs in dating science," and indeed, coaches commonly made reference to the psychology of gender, the role of kinesthetics (which they call "kino") in attraction, and ideas about gender and human evolution. As if quoting directly from the pages of *Men Are from Mars, Women Are from Venus*, coaches explained that men and women are programmed differently, a fact that must be recognized in order for heterosexual attraction to work. They offered several examples of these differences: men know right away if they are attracted to women, but women's desire builds in response to social cues;[22] men just want to be happy all the time and live in the "high," but women want a fuller range of emotions and a compelling journey; men are "hunters" who measure success by external accomplishment, whereas women measure experiences by their emotional depth; men want to solve problems and be heroes, but women want to be heard and to share intimate experiences. Coaches asserted that the science of "kino" has shown that men who want to avoid getting trapped in the friend zone must touch women early on in their interaction, slowly transitioning from friendly to sexualized forms of touch. They must place their hands on women's backs and arms to move women through space and walk women away from their friends to the bar or to the dance floor because these kinds of smaller movements establish men's leadership and lay the groundwork for later movement from the club to a new location—like his apartment—for sex. For coaches to draw so heavily on scientific and corporate lingo—kinesthesiological data, best practices, strategy, leadership, and so on—may seem unsexy, but coaches believe that these are "male languages" that resonate powerfully with their clientele.

Trainees learned how to escalate sexual touch—lifting women up, locking arms around them, tugging slightly on their pants, pulling women's bodies toward them. During a debriefing of the previous night's infield training at a club, one man shared that at first he felt shy and discouraged, but then, he said, "later in the night, I made a girl laugh about how young she was. I told her, 'I have socks older than you,' and I pulled her pants and she loved it. She gave me her number, we texted, and we've made a date to go dancing next week." The coaches congratulated him for being "on fire," using kino successfully, and getting "in state" (i.e., that nothing-to-lose frame of mind that allows men to approach women they would otherwise find intimidating). Coaches at the Love Systems training also recommended additional self-help reading—*Psycho Cybernetics* by Maxwell Maltz and *The Way of the Superior Man* by David Deida—to support students in embracing their full masculine power and potential.

Seduction students also learned how to "bypass" what coaches argued is women's culturally ingrained resistance to sex with men and tap into their "primal" arousal response. In one promotional email I received from Love Systems, aimed at selling students access to a video about "stealth" methods of seduction, trainees were promised information based on discoveries gleaned from both CIA psychological operations and neurological research from Harvard. Some of the text from the email read, "The research team at Harvard university has made a brand-new discovery involving 'Mirror Neurons' that . . . combines the latest developments in the fields of sexual psychology and unconscious communication to create sexual and emotional desire in women, regardless of the guy's age, looks, social status or personality type. . . . [Our video] shows you how to bypass a woman's rejection mechanism . . . and force-feed feelings of attraction, lust and desire directly into her subconscious mind. [It's] a system that's so subtle, it's impossible for women to even notice you're doing it to them." The promotional materials went on to explain to the men who purchase the video, "[You will learn how to] covertly slip a few innocent words into your everyday conversation with women and within seconds have them turned on, attracted to you, and ready to go."

Seduction trainers also drew on pop-sociological accounts of the way that social norms constrain heterosexual attraction, disadvantaging women and intensifying the need for men to take charge. Nick Savoy sounded irritated but resigned to these constraints when he told me, "It sucks that women feel like they have to pretend they don't want sex, but I'm not sure what we can do about that. We can only teach men to work around it." Referring again to the obstacles that slut-shaming poses for straight women's sex lives, another Love Systems coach told the trainees, "Sex is not a prize handed out by women to men. Women love sex just as much if not more [than men do]. The societal messages mislead us. Movies suggest that [women aren't as interested in sex as men], and it's not true. But a woman can't just go home with a guy. She has to feel like it was out of her control, not of her own volition. . . . You're both trying to get to the bedroom, but you have to take on the burden of responsibility."

I certainly agreed with this critique of the heteropatriarchal notion that straight women are sexual gatekeepers by nature or hard-wired to trade sex for emotional connection or "keepers of virtue" who, over the course of their lives, bestow sex—as a gift—on a select and fortunate group of lust-filled men. But I cringed at his conclusion: women, as a result of patriarchy, can only express their sexual desire through a performance of surrender, a reluctant participation in theatrical scenes in which sex is controlled by, and for the benefit of, men. Rachel O'Neill expresses a similar concern that this view of women having a strong but socially repressed sex drive causes seduction trainees to paradoxically believe that challenging a woman's "last minute resistance" is a means of honoring women's sexual impulses.[23] In the seduction industry, acknowledging women as sexual agents does little to intervene in long-standing claims that women say no when they actually mean yes.

Coaches maintained their stance that seduction students were learning to better understand the world through women's eyes, going on to declare that the answer to the question "What do women want?" is . . . a bit of masculine danger. Describing a technique that men can use to escalate sexual attraction, a coach said, "Tell her, 'If I get alone with you, it's going to be bad news for you, honey.' Don't be the nice guy. A girl is going to sleep with you either because she loves you or because she fuckin' hates you. It's like she's getting back at you. . . . You can even make rapey jokes, like hand her a drink and say, 'Oh wait, that's mine! Now *I* have the drink with the roofie in it!'" This kind of hetero-erotic narrative may not lead to rape itself but arguably has its place on the same slippery slope that the feminist psychologist Nicola Gavey has termed the "cultural scaffolding for rape."[24] How are men to distinguish between, on the one hand, straight women who want sex but feel societal pressure to pretend that they don't (i.e., to create the appearance that they are purely accommodating men's sexual desires) and, on the other hand, straight women who do not want to have sex with a given man but consent to his sexual requests because doing so yields other things that straight women want (safety, making nice, getting it over with, money, straight privilege, etc.)?

For many straight men, it seems not to matter which of these scenarios is at play, but within the context of seduction training, male trainees are led to believe that they are not taking anything from women that women don't genuinely want to give. They are trained to understand that men and women want the same sexual outcome but that men must take the lead, push a little, and allow women to perform the sexual passivity expected of them. In the name of giving straight women what they really want, men learn that what women want can never be directly communicated and therefore must be assumed—often based on the most crass and simplistic interpretations of already-questionable research on the neurological, bioevolutionary, and socially constructed differences between men and women. Differences among straight women themselves—their different sexual desires and their varying capacities to take charge of sex—get flattened out, if not ignored altogether.

Exemplifying this kind of broad generalizing about straight women, Kezia Noble announced during her bootcamp, in a salty and mocking tone, "Oh, he was so nice, I just had to have sex with him. . . . No woman has ever said that!" She went on to sing the praises of the bad-boy archetype: "If you are the bad guy, brilliant. He gives women a purpose, a challenge. He shows the world that he's a big, bad, nasty guy but he shows the woman his good sides. He has a picture of his mother by his bedside table. He has cried in front of her. She wants to save him and melt his icy heart." As I watched men take notes on this most nauseatingly heteronormative of monologues, I struggled not to roll my eyes with queer repulsion. It was not that I believed her to be wrong across the board; I knew many straight women, and queer women too, who were attracted to this kind of edgy masculinity. But it was the context of heteronormativity—wherein utterly mediocre straight men, including self-destructive, emotionally deficient tough guys, had the power to absorb straight women's attention, to make women labor to save them, to impress women with the most basic displays of human feeling—that depressed me. Here was evidence of the power and resilience of narratives that repackage men's deficiencies as enticing challenges for women.

## The Transformation: Seduction Goes New Age, Pop-Feminist, and Global

I wrapped up my fieldwork inside the seduction bootcamps in 2014, during a time now understood to be the height of the industry. In that year, I counted over fifty seduction companies based in the United States, the United Kingdom, Germany, Croatia, India, South Africa, and the Philippines, with new seduction coaches opening shop—virtually, in person, or both—at a rapid pace. Many of these companies specialized in specific strategies, such as "day game," or how to seduce women during the day at ordinary and desexualized locations like coffee shops and bookstores; others focused on specific populations, such as Asian men or older men. Some companies had names that made clear their focus on sex and dating and that retained the association with "pickup" (such as Attraction Academy, Simple Pickup, Art of the Pickup, Absolute Power Dating, Asian Dating Superstars, and Sinns of Attraction); others had names like Alpha Confidence, Charisma Arts, and Love Systems that evoked personal growth more generally. Though most companies were based in United Kingdom and the United States, many offered trainings in major cities around the world, especially where the seduction community was popular (like Rio, Melbourne, Mexico City, Tokyo, Athens, Budapest, Beijing, Bucharest, and Cape Town). Some companies offered live trainings, which could be weekend-long (at a price tag of $3,000–$4,000) or even more immersive, months-long experiences (up to $20,000), but many provided their customers primarily with online resources: apps, books, newsletters, webinars, phone coaching, and membership in wingman forums (or forums of other supportive men learning game).

When I returned to this project in 2017, the cultural terrain had shifted significantly. Both Love Systems and Kezia Noble's company (now simply called "Kezia: Celebrity Dating Coach for Men") were going strong, offering multiple bootcamps per month across Europe, Canada, and the United States. But many of the other, more salacious and openly misogynistic companies seemed to have disappeared or re-branded themselves entirely. The journalist Sarah Ratchford observed this shift in a 2017 article she wrote for *Vice*: "[Pickup artists] figured regularly in headlines until 2014, but by the end of that year they seemed to have been scrubbed from regular annals of cultural consciousness. . . . Where have these cretins gone? . . . Many pickup artists themselves are now refuting involvement with the community: Ross Jeffries, a forefa-ther of the movement, now strenuously insists that he be referred to as a 'transformational healer and thinker' instead. . . . In a world where overt misogyny is at least slightly less publicly tolerable, the relevance [of] these men is . . . questionable at best."[25] As mentioned previously, the industry received a spate of bad press in 2014, particularly with Real Social Dynamics owner Julien Blanc, an American, being banned from Australia and the United Kingdom (his visa was revoked in response to protests)[26] and dubbed the "Most Hated Man in the World" by *Time* following the release of video footage showing Blanc promoting sexual assault.[27] Ratchford also notes that pickup-artist subculture died down just as Tinder was coming into widespread usage, speculating that the hookup app may be the new stomping ground for men who once set out to seduce women at the club ("Could your average dick pic-sending Tinder bro be the new PUA?," she asks).[28]

But the fact that many of these coaches and their companies have not closed down but rather have reinvented themselves is an important part of the story of heterosexual seduction—a story impossible to tell now without attention to the #metoo movement and its effects on the way straight men are understanding casual sex. Julien Blanc, for one, had always called Real Social Dynamic a "dating coaching, self-actualization & social dynamics company" rather than a pickup-artist company, but following the global criticism of his misogyny, he stopped offering se-duction bootcamps and started offering New Age wellness seminars.

He renamed his courses "Transformation Mastery," opened them up to women, and shifted the content to meditation, deep breathing, emotional release, and healing old psychological wounds—all aimed at finding "true happiness and authenticity." Video clips on his website show mostly men but a couple of women, screaming with rage, sobbing loudly, roaring and barking like animals, and holding hands (with a yoga-ready soundtrack of New Age music playing in the background)— looking much like a hyperemotive version of Tony Robbins's "Date with Destiny" seminars described in chapter 2. According to Ratchford, Ross Jeffries—the longtime pickup artist on whom Tom Cruise purportedly based his egomaniacal pickup-artist character in the film *Magnolia*— has also drawn on New Age rhetorical devices to rebrand himself as a "transformational healer."[29] Under feminist scrutiny, seduction coaches tamped down their focus on conquering women and instead amplified their focus on healing men. But this approach, too, takes its cues right from the old mythopoetic men's movement of the 1980s and 1990s, which sought to help men rediscover their lost masculinity through spiritual healing with other men and with a strong dose of antifeminist woman-blaming thrown in for good measure.[30]

The spiritually oriented transformation of the seduction industry signals a broader tension in the ongoing reproduction of heteromasculinity. As straight men work to avoid exploiting women, sexually and otherwise, they also reify masculinity, recasting its power as the power to do good rather than bad, to protect rather than harm. Project Rockstar, a newer offshoot of Love Systems, exemplifies this kinder, gentler iteration of the seduction industry and its efforts to remake masculinity by returning men to their true essence. Rockstar is an intensive, ten-week program designed to help men completely transform their lives—to improve their game, yes, but also to transform their professional lives and even their bodies. Participants who can afford the $20,000 price tag travel across the globe together, live in different cities together, work out together, go to clubs together, and receive guidance from business mentors, wealthy entrepreneurs, nutritionists, fashion consultants, and

**Figures 3.3.** The rebranding of Julian Blanc, from 2014 and 2017.

an entire team dedicated to their holistic self-improvement. As a result, these men claim to cultivate a more refined and gentlemanly, but none-theless powerful, masculinity than is offered at traditional weekend-long seduction bootcamps.

As I began to follow Project Rockstar livestreams, I noted that the instructors were younger, more conventionally attractive, more racially diverse, and more familiar with feminist discourse than were most of seduction coaches I had studied previously. In January 2018, I received an email from Andrew, a young Asian American instructor for the company, announcing that he was going to colead "an emergency livestream about the #metoo movement" in which he would teach men "how you can talk to women without making them feel like you're the next Harvey Weinstein." I tuned in to a discussion that, despite many flaws, ended up being one of the more feminist-adjacent things I'd heard out of the mouths of straight men in some months. Somehow, in a space that had a few years ago seemed to me like one of the most misogynistic corners of the internet, young men who had come together to improve their "game" were standing up for #metoo, thinking beyond consent to consider the *quality* of women's sexual experiences, and using spot-on metaphors to help each other conceptualize good, humanizing sex. The following is an excerpt from the Project Rockstar #metoo livestream:

ANDREW: Sex should be a win/win. If you can walk away from a cir-
cumstance with a girl, it should always feel like a win/win. And thank
god we have each other in Project Rockstar to talk about this and
learn. I honestly believe that . . . you can have everyone walk away
feeling positive, that it was additive, [so] the girl doesn't feel like you
took something from her.

ALEX: Yeah, I tell girls directly, "I would never want you to do anything
you feel uncomfortable with." . . . I think it's important for girls to know
they can always get out of an uncomfortable situation. Having sex with
a girl . . . is not the goal. It's not the right place to come from. . . . Ideally
we're building guys into a place where they don't really need that gray
area where you have to push her and maybe she will feel bad about
what happened. . . . At the end of the day, women can feel when you are
trying to take something from them. Then it doesn't feel right anymore
because she sleeps with a guy and goes home and feels, "All he wanted
was to take something from me, and I gave it, and it doesn't feel good."
It's not always like an assault but just the general *feel* of the interaction.
It's like talking to a used-car sales guy. No one would say he is assaulting you, but you feel . . . that he wants you to buy this shitty car.

ANDREW: You have to see the world from women's perspective. . . . One
of the things we did [in Project Rockstar] is go to the Tony Robbins
seminar, and one of the questions he asked was, "How many women
have felt unsafe walking through a parking garage?" I shit you not,
it was every woman in the room. . . . Most guys don't realize this,
but safety is a continual and ongoing concern for women from the
moment they are a young adult until the day they die. . . . Statistically
speaking, the group of people who are most likely to harm women
is men. And so just kind of absorb that for a second, that this is the
reality most women go through. . . . The second you can understand
this . . . and empathize, that is the biggest game-changer to your game
ever. If you can recognize that women feel unsafe and make them feel
safe when they are with you, that's everything. #Metoo exists for a reason. It is an outcry against sexual assault. That's a very positive thing.

**Figure 3.4**. Alex and Andrew's "toxic masculinity" livestream.

These "Rockstars" elevated the conversation about #metoo far beyond what most male politicians and many snarky journalists had to say about women and sexual consent in 2018. In the context of President Donald Trump's "pussy grabbing," their analysis seemed almost feminist. They recognized, just as Rebecca Traister illuminated in her incisive essay about "why sex that's consensual sex can still be bad,"[31] that women often feel used or dehumanized by heterosexual sex, even during sex to which they have consented. They knew their goal was to make sure that women came to the sexual encounter, and left the sexual encounter, feeling like enthusiastic and equal contributors.

But where does this more advanced analysis, this genuine interest in women's safety and happiness, come from? Andrew argued later in the livestream that it is anchored in men's ability to access their true masculinity. "The culture of Rockstar is to be a very open and masculine man," Andrew stated. "A lot of it is about expanding yourself as a man, exploring your limits, improving yourself. But when it comes to game, as your most masculine free self, you are available to have authentic conversations with women on an energy basis, a chemistry basis, a masculine/feminine polarity basis." Similarly, one year later, following the January 2019 airing of Gillette's Super Bowl commercial critiquing toxic masculinity, Andrew and Alex offered a livestream to address their students' confusion about what constitutes toxic masculinity and how it differs from healthy expressions of masculine strength and leadership. Both men were emphatic in their assertion that sexual objectification and mistreatment of women occur when boys and men have not been taught how to properly express the "ancient, sacred" energy of masculinity, which complements, rather than harms, women. As Alex explained to his listeners, "The biggest thing you can do to make sure you have no conflict with masculinity is to ask yourself if you are treating women like an object or a person. If you are treating women like an object, you are *not* in touch with your masculinity."

These arguments bring to mind the long-running "My Strength Is Not for Hurting" campaign by Men Can Stop Rape,[32] an admirable project led by feminist men but also an example of the fact that, apparently, one of the most effective strategies for getting straight men on board with profeminist, antirape messages is giving them space to celebrate their masculinity in the same breath. From a queer perspective, this is one of the more discouraging elements of the heterosexual tragedy: when straight men move toward feminism, they almost always do so in ways that prop up the gender binary that causes their problems in the first place! Straight men's feminism—when anchored in gender-essentialist ideas about "real manhood"—also relies on the emotional labor of straight women who are compelled to celebrate and reward men for putting their "masculine energy" or "male strength" to a nonviolent use.

Another revealing account of transformation of the heterosexual-repair industry comes from Nawaz, a young Bangladeshi immigrant and graduate of Project Rockstar. Again I had received an email from Andrew, this time announcing a podcast titled "Can Brown Guys Pick Up Women Too?," in which listeners would hear the "legendary" story of a young immigrant who came to the United States, "found himself on

Rockstar [and] walked away from the program with an understanding of masculinity that far exceeds the average man's." During the podcast, Nawaz described his culture shock after moving to the United States. He explained why he pursued Project Rockstar: "[I wanted] to hook up with all these hot chicks I'd heard so much about before, but I get there, and I'm like, 'I have no skills whatsoever!'" Rehearsing the same fantasy I had heard from many trainees—both men of color and white men—Nawaz told Andrew that he wanted to be able to have sex with "tall, blond, white chicks": "That's what I was always after. That's what I'm still after." Striking a different mood from that of the #metoo livestream, Andrew chuckled and said, "Yeah, I mean, you were the typical brown guy that wanted to come to America to get the hotter chicks!"

The two men proceeded to discuss Nawaz's "amazing transformation" into a successful seducer of blond women, a transformation that Nawaz credited to learning the real meaning of masculinity:

> [At first] I was following a lot of stuff I was finding online—um, just a lot of weird stuff, a lot of pickup stuff . . . [where men are] having fun with the women but they are not masculine with the women. . . . But in Mykonos [during Project Rockstar], I realized that the skill that I had developed was next to useless because the girls [in Mykonos] don't speak English all that well. . . . So it's very difficult to [use] humor when there's not that much communication going on. In hindsight, I think that was the best thing that could've happened to me. . . . I was lacking so much masculinity. But [then I learned] to just stare in girls' eyes and just let the silence be there. The way girls would look at me completely changed. . . . It changed to what the guys call "Bambi eyes," where the girls just look at you with these really big eyes, like, really into you.

Nawaz offered a narrative about the evolution of masculinity that appears in other Project Rockstar promotional materials. While pickup artists may have relied on jokey one-liners and cocky gimmicks twenty years ago, today's game is about exuding a more reserved and sophisticated masculinity, an irresistible merging of male strength with a worldly, near-feminist respect for women. As Andrew described it, Project Rockstar cultivates "a more confident, strong foundation of masculinity," and it is this kind of masculinity that holds the power to create "win/win" sexual encounters that provide women with space to build their own desire. In this view, if men learn to perfect their masculinity, no manipulation is necessary; the doors become wide open for women to fully inhabit their own desiring bodies, to look men up and down with Bambi eyes.

Nawaz's story illuminates the role played by the seduction industry in the global recirculation of white-supremacist, heteropatriarchal constructions of women's sexual desirability. American and British seduction coaches invite and normalize the fetishization of white women's bodies. They all but promise white women to male trainees, men for whom sexual access to "hot blondes" symbolizes not only heteromasculine success but also successful assimilation as an immigrant and/or the achievement of a cosmopolitan masculinity. A desire for blond women was actively produced in Nawaz, who had already "heard so much" about the "hot chicks in the United States," a narrative that was reinforced by Andrew, an Asian American coach who described this kind of colonial, sex-driven migration as a "typical" story. Though Nawaz did not directly state whether he had participated in the pickup community in Bangladesh, it is quite possible that he had; Bangladeshi men can encounter the seduction industry and its idealization of young, white women at local, "underground" pickup-artist meetings held in Dhaka. In the full livestreamed conversation between Andrew and Nawaz, Nawaz made clear that he had spent years in the pickup community, slowly graduating from online self-study to short-term classes to the immersive Rockstar experience. This multilevel education in a seduction curriculum, produced by (mostly white) men in the United States and the United Kingdom, culminates in a striking reversal of the colonial sex tourism documented by many feminist scholars.[33] Instead of producing pathways for white men from the global North to travel to the global South in pursuit of sex with exoticized people of color, seduction coaches create pathways for men living in Asia, Africa, and Latin America to take a sex-themed tour through Europe and the United States (Rockstar participants travel from the United States to Greece to Hungary to Sweden, largely on a quest for blond women).

In this way, the seduction industry sells straight men the opportunity to participate in a global homosociality, in which access to sex with white women becomes the foundation of cross-racial and cross-national solidarity and "love" among men. As if taken right from the pages of Eve Sedgwick's analysis of what she famously termed the "erotic triangle," wherein sex with women serves to strengthen the bonds of men,[34] Nawaz described in his interview how he learned to love other men by witnessing their success seducing hot women:

> He [a fellow Rockstar student] grabbed this one girl, who was just so smoking hot. . . . I had this huge gush of jealously flow through me. . . . I think that was the first time I caught it when it was happening. Instead of focusing on him and the girl, I started focusing on what I had with a Rockstar fellow of mine I had spent the last seven weeks with. And all the memories of us having fun in Budapest and Mykonos and all throughout Vegas came to my mind. And from a place of jealously, I quickly went to a place of "I hope he bangs this chick tonight because she's smoking hot. That would be really good for him, and if he could do it, that would just make me so happy." And I wasn't just saying this. I actually felt it. . . . At that moment . . . my love for him was bigger than any form of jealousy I could have.

In Nawaz's narrative, as in many of the stories that men tell about their personal transformations in the seduction community, the romance lies not in the relationships men have with women—which are described in more transactional terms (the win/win)—but in the relationships they have with one another.[35]

Threads of race- and racism-consciousness run through the seduction curriculum, but this consciousness is as instrumental—designed to facilitate heterosexual sex—as are its gestures at empathic identification with women. Seduction coaches go to great lengths to create a shame-free environment in which men can freely express nearly any sexual desire—from quick access to "high-quality pussy" to the search for a "potential wife," from young girls with big boobs to adult women with life experience or money, from white blondes to the occasional fetish for Asian women. With regard to men's erotic aspirations, seduction trainers relate to racialized desires as neutral preferences, giving no attention to the way that the desire for young, white, blond women is shaped by relations of power, the nexus of white supremacy and misogyny.[36] Yet when it comes to circumventing *women's* racialized desires, race is indeed addressed within pickup routines, becoming fodder for playful banter and another tactic that trainees can use to surprise or "neg" the women they hope to seduce. When seduction coaches teach Asian men to approach white women and say, "Hey, just cause I'm Asian, you're not going to talk to me?" they give students permission to playfully confront white women's racism, to use white women's potential shame or defensiveness about racism as a pathway toward sex. When seduction coaches suggest that a non-Black man approaching a Black woman might say, "So what part of Korea are you from? North? South?" they teach students to immediately address the racial difference between them but in way that draws attention away from her Blackness and toward the "joke" of his mistake, a tactic that quickly defaults to the kind of color-blind and lighthearted flirtation that coaches believe works best.

## The Tragedy Continues

An enduring feature of the tragedy of heterosexuality is straight men's sense of entitlement to women's sexual and emotional service. Numerous sociological and journalistic accounts of this entitlement have documented the rage and anxiety men experience when their sexual expectations are not met—a rage that, when taken to its most violent end, has resulted in mass murder.[37] Women's sexual disinterest triggers not only anger in men but also a kind of heteropatriarchal melancholy: a sexual loss that is difficult for straight men to mourn because it is perceived to be unnatural and shameful, a denial of men's very birthright as men. As seduction coaches made clear in their interviews with me, this heteromasculine shame—and the limited number of spaces in which men believe they can express it without judgment—produced a demand for new forms of repair. Pickup-artist subculture, seduction coaches, incel communities, and Men Going Their Own Way emerged as popular homosocial sites of heterosexual repair, spaces in which the much-ignored misogyny paradox—how do you seduce women if you hate women?—could be addressed out in the open.

Like many personal and relational crises of the twenty-first century, men's heterosexual misery has been met with a neoliberal intervention—a multilevel industry offering an array of packaged services that monetize men's ability to seduce previously off-limits women by performing feminist empathy and seeing the world from "women's point of view." This instrumental approach to humanizing women certainly gives men some rudimentary training in recognizing and disavowing sexism. I, myself, have used this approach in large "Introduction to Gender and Sexuality Studies" classes, suggesting to straight male students that if for no other reason, they should at least embrace feminism because doing so will result in better heterosexuality—more authentic relationships with women and better sex based on women's enthusiastic interest, rather than women's placating and ambivalent consent. But I don't feel good about this approach; I want men to be feminists because they value women's humanity, because they identify with women, and because they see that the gender binary is a historical, political-economic, and cultural invention that has caused no end of suffering for women and also for themselves. When men extend empathy and subjectivity to women out of self-interest, to grease the wheels of sexual access or to continue receiving women's emotional labor, this makes no intervention into men's profound sense of entitlement to women's bodies and women's love, nor does it pose any challenge to men's unrelenting attachment to their own masculinity as the core of their identity, the foundation of their goodness, the basis on which they connect with other men, and the primary contribution they think they're making to the world.

# 4

# A SICK AND BORING LIFE

## Queer People Diagnose the Tragedy

I'm going on record here to notify every heterosexual male and female that every lesbian and every homosexual is all too aware of the problems of heterosexuals since they permeate every aspect of our social, political, economic, and cultural lives. . . . I think all of us are authorities on the heterosexual problem.
—Jill Johnston

Once you're on this track, you're pretty much a lesbian and you think like a lesbian and you live with lesbians and your community is lesbians, and the heterosexual world is foreign.
—Gloria Anzaldúa

IN MANY YEARS OF TEACHING AT UC RIVERSIDE, I'VE noticed that the queer kids—almost all of them young people of color—tend to sit together in my courses, often forming a boisterous and gorgeously gender-diverse queer zone in the front two rows of the lecture hall. This huddling together is about their comfort, safety, and connectedness to one another and not about me, and yet I do sometimes experience it as a protective shield for myself, a shield between my place at the podium—standing there alone, a forty-five-year-old white dyke who can still feel like a vulnerable queer kid—and the three hundred other students who might not be receptive to the tidal wave of intersectional feminism that my courses send their way. Educators have a good idea by now why all the queer kids—or any other marginalized group of students—are huddling together; as Beverly Daniel Tatum demonstrated in her groundbreaking 1997 book *Why Are All the Black Kids Sitting Together in the Cafeteria?*, self-segregation is a wise and powerful coping strategy for kids who are underrepresented and unsafe in their learning environments.[1] We know, too, that this coping strategy extends into adulthood, when we still need comfort and safety, and is part of what drives the development of racial, immigrant, and sexual enclaves. If we want to know why many queer people prefer their own company to the company of straights, certainly one answer to this question is about protection and mutual care—we hold each other up in a world that pushes us down.

But there is also another, far less discussed facet to this story about queer people keeping their distance from straight people—an element that has less to do with queer vulnerability or oppression in the face of straight privilege and more to do with queer power, freedom, abundance or relief in the face of heterosexual misery and myopia. It is a story about queer people sometimes finding straight culture and relationships too sad or enraging to witness, too boring or traumatic to endure. It is about queers often wishing to look away from the train wreck, by which I mean the seemingly inextricable place of sexual coercion and gender injustice within straight culture, or what the feminist writer JoAnn Wypijewski described in 2013—as she reflected on the ubiquity of sexual assault among teenagers—as heterosexuality's relentlessly "primitive" attachment to lies, manipulation, and violence as the formative route to sex.[2] It is about queer recoil, or something like the nausea that the French scholar Paul Preciado has felt in response to both the aesthetics and the misery (the miserable aesthetics?) of heterosexuality, described in an essay titled "Letter from a Transman to the Old Sexual Regime": "I am as far removed from your aesthetics of heterosexuality as a Buddhist monk levitating in Lhassa is from a Carrefour supermarket. . . . It doesn't excite me to 'harass' anyone. It doesn't interest me to get out of my sexual misery by touching a woman's ass on public transport. . . . The grotesque and murderous aesthetics of necro-political heterosexuality turns my stomach."[3] Sometimes straight culture is quite literally repulsive; we feel it in the gut.

We have insufficient language to describe queer people's experience of finding straight culture repellent and pitiable, given that heterosexuality has been presented to us as love's gold standard. But even without a suitable name for this contradiction—the fact that the world's most glorified relationship is often a miserable one—many queers have still spoken this truth. In 1984, a few years before his death, James Baldwin explained to an interviewer from the *Village Voice* that queers could see the precarity of heterosexuality, even as straights kept it hidden from themselves: "The so-called straight person is no safer than I am really. . . . The terrors homosexuals go through in this society would not be so great if society itself did not go through so many terrors it doesn't want to admit."[4] As Baldwin saw it, it is not simply that straight people are suffering and in denial about it but that heterosexual misery expresses itself through the projection of terror onto the homosexual.

One way to think about this is that homophobia is the outward expression of heterosexual misery, a kind of subconscious jealous rage against the gendered and sexual possibilities that lie beyond the violence and disappointments of straight culture. Added to this anger is also an unspoken sadness—a chilling cloud of resignation—that is a palpable and sometimes repellent ingredient of the affect of straight culture. Straight people have few opportunities to grieve the disappointments of straight culture (the bad and coercive sex, the normalized inequities of daily life, straight men's fragility and egomania, straight women's growing disillusionment with men's fragility and egomania, the failed marriages, the coparenting that is really solo parenting . . .) because how does one speak about the failure of the very system that defines people's success? Often the problem is described as a feminist one; it's not straightness itself but the need for men to relinquish power and privilege and reform their bad behaviors. This analysis of the problem keeps many straight women discernibly sad and angry as they trudge along in search of one of the few "good men" or labor to reform the men already in their lives, often as consumers of the heterosexual-repair industry. The Radicalesbians (Rita Mae Brown among them) called out this problem in 1970:

What is a lesbian? A lesbian is the rage of all women condensed to the point of explosion. . . . She is forced to evolve her own life pattern, . . . learning usually much earlier than her "straight" (heterosexual) sisters about the essential aloneness of life (which the myth of marriage obscures). . . . As long as woman's liberation tries to free women without facing the basic heterosexual structure that binds us in one-to-one relationship with our oppressors, tremendous energies will continue to flow into trying to straighten up each particular relationship with a man, into finding how to get better sex, how to turn his head around, into trying to make the "new man" out of him.[5]

Indeed, tremendous energy on the part of straight women continues to flow in the direction of repairing straight men, resulting in a lot of displaced disappointment and grief for which queer people (the gay or lesbian best friend) can become sounding boards and confidants. This heterofeminine grief is displaced to the extent that it remains focused on fixing relationships with individual men rather than identifying hetero norms and heteromasculinity themselves as fundamental problems. The point here is that straight people's displaced and unmournable grief, what Judith Butler has described as "heterosexual melancholy," sometimes feels, from a queer point of view, like too heavy an emotional burden to bear.[6]

The affect of straight culture is marked not only by repressed anger and sadness but by a kind of emotional flatness, an antiflamboyance. Here, straight culture and WASP culture overlap, highlighting the ways that straight people of color, Jews, Muslims, people with disabilities, sluts, fat people, and white queers—to name a few—depart from the norms associated with straightness and/or whiteness. For example, a common straight critique of gay affect in the mid- and late twentieth century was that it was too flamboyant—too spectacular, too loud, too sexual, too confident, too animated, too exposed, and overall just too much. If we reverse the gaze, focusing on queer people's assessment of the look and feel of straight life, we can see how straight people—

especially straight white people—might seem to queers too passive, boring, unimaginative, and generally uninspired. If queerness is too much,
then straightness is too little, the relational manifestation of lack. Let us
not forget that "straight" was originally something of an insult, a slang
term first used by gay men in the mid-twentieth century to describe men
who had once been sexually fluid but had returned, at least temporarily,
to the confines of a straight and narrow life.[7] The use of "straight" as an
insult continued into the 1960s and '70s among hippies, self-identified
freaks, and counterculture enthusiasts who used the term to describe
the stifling and uninspired quality of mainstream American life. A 1967
*Time* magazine article titled "The Hippies: Philosophy of a Subculture"
testified to the responsibility of every freak to help reform straight people by describing the hippie credo as follows: "Leave society as you have
known it. Leave it utterly. Blow the mind of every straight person you
can reach. Turn them on, if not to drugs, then to beauty, love, honesty,
fun."[8] Concern and anger about straight life persisted well into the 1990s,
as activists in Queer Nation pointed to the fragility and obliviousness of
straight people who feared homosexuality and celebrated heteronormative rituals at every turn with seemingly no concern for the precarity of
queer life, especially at the height of the AIDS epidemic (see figure 4.1).

To return to my "queer kids sitting together in the classroom" metaphor, we might also consider that sometimes queer kids huddle together
because they know, or at least imagine, that the other kids, the straight
kids, have little or nothing to offer them. As Wypijewski asserts, "It is
a common fallacy for any majority group to believe that a minority's
struggle for equality signals a wish to be just like the majority. . . . [But]
heteros have nothing to teach homos beyond, maybe, how to endure
childbirth, [while] the opposite—that heteros have something to learn,
from the history of gay liberation, . . . is surely true."[9] And, in a *HuffPost*
article titled "Why I Never Want to Be Just Like Straight People," Noah
Michelson explains it this way: "From where I'm standing, it seems that
straight people haven't done so hot when it comes to love, sex, marriage,
the family or gender roles, among other things. So why would I want to

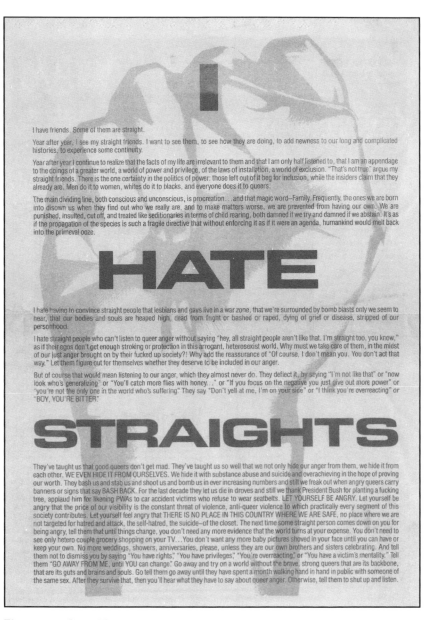

**Figure 4.1.** Queer Nation poster.

buy into that dysfunctional system?"[10] In other words, the queer kids may be sitting together not because they are patiently waiting to be invited to participate in straight culture (i.e., what we might call a politics of *inclusion*) but because they have no interest in what straight culture has to offer (i.e., a politics of *refusal*).

I gather that not all queers refuse straight culture, but this chapter is about queer people who do. It is about clarifying for straight people that many of us are not longing for access to heterosexual traditions but feeling very troubled by straight people's denial about their own gendered suffering. I know this about queer people because the queer people in my life—comrades, students, friends, colleagues—commonly bemoan what is sad, boring, stifling, and uninspired about straight life. This is not to suggest that queerness is any kind of multicultural safe harbor from systemic injustice, of course. Many queer subcultures, like straight culture, are built on intersecting forms of violence: anti-Blackness, misogyny, transphobia, ableism, and economic injustice. Queer and trans people of color refuse white queer culture and its endemic racism; queer feminists refuse queer misogyny and femme-phobia and its long-standing place within gay culture. But within many queer people's own particular queer worlds (Black and Brown queer worlds, trans queer worlds, feminist queer worlds), in the safest spaces we can fashion for ourselves with other QTPOC folks, feminists, kink communities, and so on, we look out at the tragedy of heterosexuality, and many of us feel gratitude to have escaped it. Queer people of color may not feel any affinity with queer white people, for instance, but they may feel strong political and cultural alignments with other queer and trans people of color and have significant critiques of (and often alienation from) heterosexual people of color—even as strategic alliances among all people of color are essential to fighting and surviving white supremacy. In other words, taking queerness seriously as a cultural formation distinct from straight culture does not obscure hierarchies among queer people. It allows us to sharpen our powers of intersectional analysis, noting how queerness results in different kinds of group affiliation and practice.

To illuminate queer people's perceptions of the tragedy of hetero-sexuality, I put out multiple calls on social media (Facebook and Twitter) for queer-identified people in my extended social network—my queer friends, colleagues, comrades, students, acquaintances, friends of friends—to complete a very brief survey that asked them two direct questions (in addition to asking about their racial/ethnic and gender identity): "1. In general, all else being equal, do you prefer the company of queer-identified people over straight-identified people? Why or why not? 2. Is there anything about straight people, or straight culture, that you find off-putting? Uncomfortable? Sad? Strange? Tell me about it." I received fifty-eight substantive responses: thirty from queer-identified people of color and twenty-eight from queer-identified white people.[11] Of these, four respondents answered no to both questions, remarking that they had fulfilling relationships with straight people, did not prefer the company of queers, and felt no sense of alienation from straight culture; two answered yes, they prefer queer people's company, but no, they don't find anything off-putting about straight culture; and the rest, the remaining fifty-three people who kindly agreed to answer my questions, replied with a resounding yes and yes.

I want to be 100 percent clear about the intimate, nonscientific, and nonrepresentative nature of the ideas presented in this chapter. Clearly, this is not a "representative sample" of LGBT people; speaking on behalf of all queer people, or representing a very broad array of perspectives, is not my goal. Instead, I imagine this chapter is more like an invitation to a large queer, trans, feminist, multiracial, intergenerational dinner party (with fifty-eight people!) in which guests have been asked to participate in a critical discussion about straight culture. Personally, as a queer person, I would be thrilled to be invited to that party, but I'd probably be even more excited as a straight person to be given the opportunity to listen, with the understanding that I generally do not have access to this kind of opportunity to see, in a new and critical way, how some queer people view the cultural context in which my sexuality has been formed. This chapter should be read as an ethnography of my own social and political milieu, reflecting my feminist, queer social network and the kinds of conversations that happen within it.

I hope, too, that readers will resist the temptation to react to the critiques raised here with the response "not all straight people are like that" because, as I explained earlier, (a) no one is arguing that every single straight-identified individual is boring or abusive or bad in bed and (b) this is almost always a deflection tactic designed to shift attention away from an uncomfortable critique (see #notallmen and #notallwhitepeople as crystal-clear examples). As I have written about elsewhere, methodological critiques are also frequently used as a deflection strategy when readers feel implicated or threatened by new and/or critical ideas.[12] Beyond questions of representativeness, another methodological concern a reader might raise is whether the questions I asked were "leading" questions. In response to this concern, we might consider that whether a question is a leading question is based on a collective agreement about the taken-for-grantedness of the subject at hand. For example, questions like "What is your first and last name?" "What is your race?" and "What is your gender?" are generally not considered leading questions because we presume that most respondents have a first and last name, a racial identity, and a gender identity. But this kind of taken-for-grantedness is also deeply influenced by the political zeitgeist, as well as by the extent to which the person asking the question feels obligated to act as a seemingly objective and naïve inquisitor. To ask a group of Black respondents whether they find anything uncomfortable about white people or white culture would probably have been perceived as an offensive and leading question a few decades ago (#notallwhitepeople!) but less so today as more researchers have come to expect that systems of power, and the cultures of privilege that cohere around them, are almost assuredly going to create suffering and discomfort for subjugated people (and that subjugated people have probably noticed this and have things to say about it). In a similar regard, it is my experience—in the queer worlds I circulate in—that critical assessments of straight culture are a common, though perhaps relatively hidden, feature of what radical queers talk about

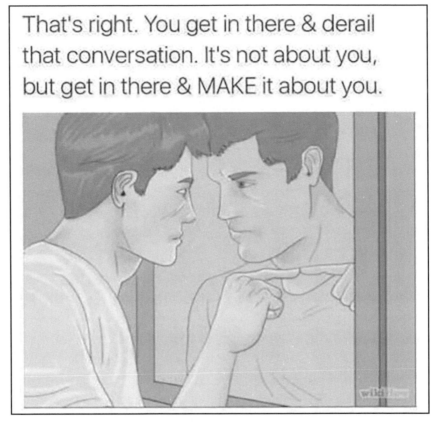

**Figure 4.2.** Many #notallmen memes appeared in 2017.

among ourselves. It can also be an uncomfortable topic for more assimi-lationist gays who care little about queer and feminist critique, though I am not interested here in that perspective. My friends and acquaintances answered with wide-ranging, concrete, and unprompted details (e.g., the remarkably frequent reference to what is "boring" about straight culture) that illuminate both their unique and shared experiences. Their responses contained complex and fascinating analyses of heterosexual suffering and wide-ranging examples of the heterosexual rituals they found most trou-bling. These narratives contribute valuable fragments to my larger story about the tragedy of heterosexuality, and I use them as witness testimony, as signposts in our tour of queer feelings about straight problems.

## The Boredom

"I often feel bored and/or alienated by straight company. It's all very predictable and uninteresting. . . . Queers have more fun without being shitty to other people (setting aside critiques of many white gay boys that I know). Which is why, I assume, so many straight people try to infiltrate queer spaces." (queer Vietnamese-American transguy)[13]

"I find straight Black folks boring. The ones I am thinking of are middle aged and upper middle class. They are boring to talk to. They tend to be pretty one-dimensional in social settings and not very concerned with the types of social justice issues that are most important to me (LGBT issues, structural racism, gender inequities)." (queer Black lesbian)

"I'm not sure why women put up with most men and their selfishness. Men tend to suck the energy out of the room and replace it all with boring vapor. They have many, many thoughts and ideas, most of them vapid." (queer, white, misandrist bitch)

"Just the normy-ness and the boring lives straight people can lead. . . . Sometimes it sucks the joy out of me." (queer Arab femme)

"I often reflect on Edith Massie's [sic] quote in John Waters's *Female Trouble*: 'the world of the heterosexual is a sick and boring life.' Probably the most obvious part is the inability for many straight couples to be honest with each other about their additional attractions. . . . I think this is sad and sews mistrust." (queer Latinx male)

"I like straight people just fine. But straight culture is dull as dirt. It isn't even culture. It's just what's left over when all the interesting stuff has been driven out." (femme WASP)

"Straight men just seem like duds, like the worst person to get stuck next to at a dinner party. They don't ever seem equally matched to their women partners—like the woman does all the socializing/connecting and the man has little to say or mansplains and interrupts or dominates." (queer white trans)

"They all do the same thing as other single or coupled straight people as if they are following a given agenda. It's uncomfortable how boring they are." (queer Hispanic female)

Back in chapter 1, I quoted from the fabulously over-the-top character Aunt Ida, played by Edith Massey in John Waters's 1974 cult film *Female Trouble*, who scolds her straight-identified nephew about being a heterosexual: "Queers are just better. I'd be so proud of you as a fag. . . . I'd never have to worry. . . . The world of heterosexuals is a sick and boring life." So too does one of the respondents above quote Aunt Ida's wise words; we both hark back to a dark and utterly bizarre film from 1974 to find corroboration for something that remains true to our present experience and yet is rarely acknowledged. Indeed, "boring" was the most frequently repeated descriptive term used by my queer interlocutors to describe straight people and/or straight culture. Things that bore us are not just uninteresting but often also often tedious, repetitive, unoriginal, mechanical, and sometimes mind numbing. To bore something is also to make a hole in it, to hollow something out; hence, sometimes being bored feels like being completely empty. Significantly, Valerie Solanas began *SCUM Manifesto*, her 1967 wild feminist screed against the patriarchy, by reminding readers that oppression and boredom are interconnected: "Life in this society being, at best, an utter bore and no aspect of society being at all relevant to women, there remains to civic-minded, responsible, thrill-seeking females only to overthrow the government, eliminate the money system, institute complete automation and destroy the male sex."[14]

Queer conversations about the boredom of straight life take place with different languages and at multiple registers. In the academic realm of queer studies, the fact that straight culture feels tedious and repetitive is sometimes traced back to the way gender itself is a repetition, a never-ending process of attempting to achieve normative, or at least legible, femininity or masculinity.[15] Everyone more or less follows the same predictable scripts that signal gender success in a given time and place. Sometimes queer scholars understand the mechanical and unoriginal quality of straight culture to be reflected in its obsession with reproduction, or the ways that straight adults so often pin their own value and happiness on their children's future accomplishments—a literal reproduction of themselves.[16] Numerous queer scholars have also argued, in different ways, that heterosexuality is *intended* to be boring, its very design aimed at control and predictability. Straight culture keeps people having babies, buying products, working hard in the paid labor force to support children, and fearing many of the potentially less boring sexual desires and/or subcultural practices that are inconvenient for capitalism, white supremacy, and the state.[17]

These same problems are critiqued in queer popular culture, where queer commentators like to point out just how *basic* straight culture is. (For older readers, to be "basic" means to be a follower, to lack any special and unpredictable characteristics. As they say on Urban Dictionary, it means, for instance, drinking pumpkin spice lattes, wearing yoga pants, and watching *Keeping Up with the Kardashians* or, for straight dudes, loving sports and reading *Maxim*.) In 2018, Dayna Troisi and Corrine Werder of the lesbian magazine *GO* ("the cultural roadmap for city girls everywhere") enumerated the basic rituals of straight culture in an article titled "70 Things That Straight People Love."[18] The list—a queer take-off of the hit blog "Stuff White People Like"—included promise rings, gender-reveal parties, boat shoes, "Live, Laugh, Love" art, sip and paint events, Chinese-symbol tattoos, talking about the cut of engagement rings, gendering *everything*, cruises, voting for white supremacists,[19] royal weddings, drag queens but not drag kings, *Law and Order: SVU*, and parties for every single life event, among many other uninspired cultural preferences. Each item came with a short explanation:

- Spirit animals: I just don't understand why straight people list a dolphin as their spirit animal in their Tinder bio? Not to mention, this is racist AF.
- "Love is love": Thinking this phrase is allyship is like getting a kiddy pool to cool off on a 98 degree day. It's just not going to cut it.
- Self-help books: *The Secret* is a favorite amongst the straights.
- Men explaining beer and women thinking they're *so different* for liking beer. Straight culture at its finest.[20]

This is a fluff piece, but the authors zero in on many of the same elements of straight culture that my friends quoted above also named. The obsessive gendering, empty expressions of solidarity, mansplaining husbands and boyfriends, addiction to mainstream media and mass-marketed tchotchkes, and self-improvement programs run on delusions and/or self-loathing (especially those offered by the heterosexual-repair industry)—these are things that queers "just don't understand," according to Troisi and Werder. For context, Troisi describes herself as "a dyke princess who is passionate about sex + dating, beauty + fashion, Lana Del Rey, and her badass bionic arm," and Werder's bio says she "looks at the world through the lens of an anti-capitalist, pleasure activist, femme-of-center queer woman."[21]

There is debate among queers about how much we may be guiltily or ironically consuming some of these same straight, or normcore, fetish objects.[22] But the problem isn't really one of bad taste; it's not about the "Live, Love, Laugh" posters but about what they represent and why they are being consumed. Returning to the responses that began this section, straight people's attachments to mainstream culture and the status quo are sometimes accompanied by apathy about social justice projects, and *this* is what makes heterosexuals the worst people to get stuck next to at a dinner party. Straight culture is marked by a willful focus on keeping things light and comfortable, and primary among those more urgent subjects that straight people would rather not discuss is the *straight men problem*. As described earlier, straight men suck the energy out of the room, and straight men are the first to fill it with boring vapor. Straight culture is what's left over when all the interesting stuff has been emptied out or bored through. Straight women do the emotional labor, and straight men step in, or interrupt, when it's time to explain things. And how do queers know this? We have witnessed it, but we have also listened to straight women complain about it, which brings us to the next element of straight culture I want to discuss.

## It's Sad How Much Women and Men Dislike Each Other

"Let's talk about the sitcoms straight folks keep making for each other. Do straight couples even know they should actually LIKE each other? Because I don't think they do." (queer, white, nonbinary)

"I find straight women a bit sad, because so many of them seem to detest men, and despise the men they're with." (queer African American woman)

"Ugh, so I'm in this otherwise pretty progressive embroidery FB group, and the straight women in the group so often complain about their worthless husbands and boyfriends. These dudes are awful—no job, playing video games all day, barely speaking to their partners, not sharing chores or childcare, while women are doing ALL THE THINGS. Now, I try to empathize with people's struggles, but why dear god do these women stay with these awful dudes? It drives me nuts! . . . I really don't get it." (queer, white woman)

"Work is my life now so I spend my time with my work colleagues— mostly straight cis white guys in their 30s and 40s. There is a lot of shit talking about unsatisfied wives and midlife crisis feels. Which is incredibly sad." (queer Vietnamese-American transguy)

"Straight couples, on average, don't seem to have very much fun with each other. I frequently see men looking bored while their girlfriends chat with each other, or vice versa. . . . I see lots of articles written by frustrated wives who do more of the housework/childcare/managing of things and I wonder why they bother dating men." (queer white lesbian)

From a queer point of view, one of the defining features of straight culture is *complaint*. Straight women complain about men they date or marry with such gusto that queer people are left shaking our heads and thinking, "My god, why, why, *why* does this woman stay with someone she finds this pathetic?" In *The Female Complaint*, Lauren Berlant demonstrates that complaint was cultivated in women through the nineteenth and twentieth centuries in order to create a singular and normative "women's culture" organized around the premise that heteroromantic love is what women want most and what they will seek at all costs, even when it fails them and causes them great pain.[23] Products marketed to women—cosmetics, romantic films and literature, self-help programs—manufactured sentimental belonging in "shared womanness" by celebrating women's ability to survive their disappointing and failed relationships, and this survival became a defining feature of women's empowerment. For Berlant, the female complaint also keeps individual women tethered to their own somewhat-unique expressions of normative heterofemininity: "[Women's culture] flourishes by circulating as an already felt need, a sense of emotional continuity among women who identify with the expectation that, as women, they will manage personal life and lubricate emotional worlds. This commodity world, and the ideology of normative, generic-but-unique femininity trains women to expect to be recognizable by other members of this intimate public, even if they reject or feel ambivalent about its dominant terms."[24] By the twenty-first century, complaints about men, or the collective recognition that "men are trash" (see the ubiquitous Twitter hashtag), has become the endlessly meme-ified and T-shirt-emblazoned slogan for empowered straight ladies. As Berlant explains, this ostensibly

**Figure 4.3.** Angela Bassett surviving heterosexuality.

universal women's culture is marketed as one that spans race and class hierarchies among women, attempting to hail all American women into its membership. Indeed, to the extent that art and music by Black women has been embraced by mainstream white feminism, it has often taken the form of the sassy, resilient Black woman trope described by Melissa Harris-Perry in *Sister Citizen*.[25] Black women, already cast in the white imagination as strong, aggressive, and hyperheterosexual, come to represent the possibility that all straight women can survive bad men, a hurdle that is arguably a heteroromantic rite of passage (with an anthem by Gloria Gaynor).

Straight culture's orientation toward heteroromantic sacrifice is also influenced by socioeconomic class. Respect for sacrifice—or sucking it up and surviving life's miseries—is one of the hallmarks of white working-class culture, for instance, wherein striving for personal happiness carries less value than does adherence to familial norms and traditions.[26] Maturity and respectability are measured by what one has given up in order to keep the family system going, an ethos that is challenged by the presence of a queer child, for instance, who insists on "being who they are." Queerness—to the extent that it emphasizes authenticity in one's sexual relationships and fulfillment of personal desires—is an affront to the celebration of heteroromantic hardship. As Robin Podolsky has noted, "What links homophobia and heterosexism to the reification of sacrifice . . . is the specter of regret. Queers are hated and envied because we are suspected of having gotten away with something, of not anteing up to our share of the misery that every other decent adult has surrendered to."[27]

For many lesbian daughters of working-class straight women, opting out of heterosexuality exposes the possibility of another life path, begging the question for mothers, "If my daughter didn't have to do this, did I?" Heterosexuality is compulsory for middle-class women, too, but more likely to be represented as a gift, a promise of happiness, to be contrasted with the ostensibly "miserable" life of the lesbian. The lesbian feminist theorist Sara Ahmed has offered a sustained critique of the role of queer abjection in the production of heteroromantic fantasies. In *Living a Feminist Life*, she notes that "it is as if queers, by doing what they want, expose the unhappiness of having to sacrifice personal desires . . . for the happiness of others."[28] In the *Promise of Happiness*, Ahmed argues, "Heterosexual love becomes about the possibility of a happy ending; about what life is aimed toward, as being what gives life direction or purpose, or as what drives a story."[29] Marked by sacrifice, misery, and failure along the way, the journey toward heterosexual happiness (to be found with the elusive "good man") remains *the* journey.

Of course, any straight woman in her right mind *would* complain. As Adrienne Rich argued in 1980, "Profound skepticism, caution, and righteous paranoia about men may indeed be part of any healthy woman's response to the woman-hatred embedded in male-dominated culture." But Rich also highlighted that because misogyny is so profoundly normalized, many women, even feminist women, "fail to identify it until it takes, in their own lives, some permanently unmistakable and shattering form."[30]

The normalization of misogyny, and women's sense that although straight men are often unlikable and/or abusive, women must endure them anyway (because how else are women going to get their sexual and romantic needs met?) continues to have such cultural resonance that it is often the more or less explicit premise of self-help books marketed to women.

Notably, straight women's feminist insights, but also their related sense of resignation and hopelessness about heterosexuality, have expanded in the past thirty years since the publication of Susan Forward's 1986 self-help classic *Men Who Hate Women and the Women Who Love Them* and Robin Norwood's 1990 *Women Who Love Too Much: When You Keep Wishing and Hoping He'll Change*. While these earlier self-help best sellers presumed that good men and healthy relationships could be possible but were denied to women with low self-esteem and poor decision-making skills, more recent titles, like Blythe Roberson's 2018 book *How to Date Men When You Hate Men*, start from the feminist premise that straight women face a double bind caused not by their own emotional deficiencies but by patriarchy. Roberson asserts that, on the one hand, men are systematically oppressing women, but on the other hand, they are also hot. What to do? She identifies herself, for instance, "as a horned-up perv, . . . a woman attracted to men who have all this structural power . . . and have been told for millennia that it's cool to treat women in a very degrading way, consciously or subconsciously."[31] She goes on to wonder, "How do you date men when they don't want to date anyone more successful than they are? Why get married when marriage benefits men in almost every way but makes women more likely to die a violent death?"[32] Roberson answers these questions with a critique of romantic idealism and a willingness to embrace singleness, even as she describes her plan this way: "keep trying to get men to kiss me while not oppressing me."[33] With so much attention in these books given to straight men who hate women and straight women who hate men, it is a wonder that lesbians continue to be perceived as the ultimate man-haters. Roseanne Barr once pointed to this contradiction in one of her well-known comedy routines: "I don't know why people think lesbians hate men. They don't have to have sex with them!"[34] The joke works because people are familiar with the stereotype about lesbians hating men, but many also know, as my dyke friend Robin recently put it during one of our lesbian writing group meetings, "the real fury and vitriol directed at men does not come from lesbians but straight women."

Roberson acknowledges that she learned as a young girl that, in straight culture, "flirting" is synonymous with opposite-sex "meanness." Like Roberson, I learned this lesson too, and I still remember being told by my mother that a boy who had pushed me in elementary school probably "*liked* me." In this way, behaviors we associate with disliking someone, like intentionally hurting them, get resignified by straight culture as indicators of like, of attraction. So it's no wonder that there is no disconnect between love and complaint, no shame in men "shit talking their wives" or women staying with one of those "worthless husbands and boyfriends" they complain about on embroidery-themed Facebook pages. The dislike, dissatisfaction, complaint, and witnessing by others is part of the heteroromantic ritual, albeit one that queer people find both tragic and mind-boggling. From a queer feminist perspective, perhaps humans do sometimes have sex with people we hate, but a sexual orientation organized around mutual dislike (men's misogyny and women's resentment) is not our best vision for the future.

## Straight Men Are the Worst (and Straight Women Are Enablers)

"I can't handle how low the bar is for straight-identified men when it comes to literally everything: emotional skills, sexual skills, communication, self-awareness. When I am not annoyed or enraged about this, it makes me deeply sad." (queer femme, white, cis woman)

"Straight men and the way they treat everyone makes me uncomfortable. My guard is always fully up when I meet a new straight man. He might hurt anyone, including himself at any moment to prove how manly he is. . . . I am ready to fight for my life whenever I meet a new straight man. . . . Also the way straight women coddle and excuse away the behavior of their partners as if they are children. They are enabling them to do dumb shit." (queer Latina)

"Toxic masculinity." (queer Hispanic male)

"I find it depressing to see what my straight female friends put up with regarding treatment from men. I really sympathize with these women, but at the same time it makes me feel alienated from them. Our lives become so different when theirs revolves around attachment to a cruel, insensitive, self-centered, or simply boring man." (queer white European cis female)

"As a femme lover of female masculinities, I loathe few things more than hetero-masculinity. . . . Hetero-femininity, conversely, just saddens me. Things I find particularly loathsome about straight people: entitlement, smugness, disdain, exoticized same-sex curiosity guised as repulsion, condescension, power, capital, oblivion, perceptual dissatisfaction with 'self' masked as bourgeois self improvement, sexual repression, and straight sex." (queer woman of color of Pakistani descent)

"The gender dynamics between cis-het straight people are often disturbing and not especially feminist. Even if the man 'supports' feminism, he eats up more air time, . . . he looks for validation. . . . When I spend time with single cis-het female friends, much of the conversation is dominated by their dating lives, and sadly, pathetically, whether or not a man they are dating is ignoring them. . . . I also hate it when cis-het women say things like, 'I wish I could just be a lesbian.'" (Filipino, masculine female)

"It's wild how fragile straight masculinity can be, but also how much straight women just accept that men will not know/understand/really care about certain things about their experiences." (queer, white, gender-fluid, nonbinary)

"Heteronormativity, misogyny, transphobia, toxic masculinity, overbearing gender expectations." (queer Latina)

"Seeing brilliant straight women settle for men sooooo beneath them." (queer, white, butch)

"Straight men in particular are odd and uncomfortable to be around for me. Those insecure in their masculinity very often police mine, which manifests as gaslighting, invalidating my anxieties and 'softer' emotions. And their constant performances of 'toughness' is just very exhausting." (mixed-race Black, no gender given)

"Women would be much happier if they weren't enmeshed in the nightmare of heterosexuality. Men and society harm them in so many ways. . . . Why do people choose to be straight? I feel sorry for them." (queer white man)

"I cannot deal with straight white dudes AT ALL (the mansplaining, their privilege, their inability to feel emotions that aren't anger, their homophobia, etc). Straight women are fine, I guess, but they have so much baggage (damage) from dating and interacting with straight white dudes that it's often hard to be around them. . . . If I have to hear one more straight woman say 'my brother/husband/son is one of the good ones,' I'm probably going to punch someone." (white, queer)

"It seems straight women . . . have it pretty shitty. . . . For example, there was an article going around on Facebook that a lot of my straight female friends were posting. . . . It was an 'open letter' by a [married woman] to her husband and basically it asked him to watch the kids sometimes so she could have a break, and help her with small tasks around the house. . . . It [was] asking for basic things, so simple, I was shocked it was even an issue for this woman, let alone every straight woman I knew on Facebook." (queer white female)

The reason it is unsettling for many queers to listen to straight women complain about men's deficiencies is not because we don't agree with this assessment (we *agree*) but because it is distressing to hear these same women justify or resign themselves to men's shortcomings. The bar often seems to be set very low for straight-identified men. They express a feeling or take care of their infant or do the dishes or stop talking and recognize women's authority on a subject or give a woman an orgasm, and we are all so pleased. We are pleased because we expect so little. Straight women are especially delighted when the men they love display basic decency or reciprocity, and they tell us so: "I am so lucky to have one of the good ones," they say. Meanwhile, many of us queers are thinking, "*That's* what counts as *good*?" We also know that the answer is yes, it is what counts as good, because as the folks quoted above explain, many straight men are violent and unpredictable. They are cruel, insensitive, self-centered, and simply boring. They are entitled, smug, and condescending. They are fragile, insecure, and in regular need of women's validation. They are lazy and less competent, but more respected, than are the women in their lives. Knowing all of this, queers are braced for the inevitable moment when a straight woman proclaims, offhandedly, "I wish I could just be a lesbian." Sigh. Why don't you be one, then? some of us wonder. It's not *that* hard.

Roberson's book, discussed earlier, is a good example of straight women's structural bind. Roberson wants to say that she hates men because she recognizes hate as a logical way for straight women to feel (what's not to hate about patriarchy and its subjects?). But if she fully and sincerely claims this position, she has to quit dating men, or she has to be a person who has sex with people she hates. Neither choice appears to be an option for Roberson, and presumably many straight women, so she goes on at length about how the title of her book is actually tongue-in-cheek, because while she knows men-as-a-group are oppressing her, she *adores* individual men, "just like the suffragettes in *Mary Poppins*." Women's swirl of heteroadoration and real or performative hatred can look to queer observers like a kind of gallows humor. What can a straight woman do but laugh and/or cry about having a husband she finds lazy and thoughtless,[35] a terrible conversationalist,[36] and as much work as taking care of a child?[37]

When I was young, my mother had a woman friend who spoke regularly about how much she hated her husband. He used to blow his nose in the shower and leave mucous clogging the drain, just one of the many reasons she loathed him. I know another woman, the mother of a friend of mine, who lives in a large house with a husband who has cheated on her more than once; she sleeps on a love seat in the living room, her legs dangling off the side, because that is how little she wishes to sleep with him. I recently heard of a woman in my community who was left by her husband within days of giving birth because he "couldn't handle it" (he ultimately came back but had a nice vacation away from his newborn baby). I know a woman whose husband had an affair while she was experiencing postpartum anxiety and nursing two small children. I know a woman who shared with me that her husband's body is completely unappealing to her and that she has sex with him just to make him happy. I know a woman who is embarrassed to introduce her husband to her friends because he can't keep up with her, or them, intellectually. Another woman I know has fallen out of love with her husband because his lack of emotional presence has made her feel alone for many years. I know a woman who used to be my neighbor until her fifty-something-year-old husband started smoking weed every day, become a Grateful Dead enthusiast, and moved his girlfriend into their home to live alongside his two young children. She told me this while standing on the curb outside her house, wanting to know if I had any ideas about where she could live. I know a woman, my own mother, whose husband cheated on her multiple times, became addicted to drugs and gambling, and left her to raise two young children.

Queer observers of heterosexual misery don't always know how to feel about straight women's suffering. Perhaps it is their own private business; perhaps everything is fine as long as straight women, themselves, are willing to forgive the men in their lives. And perhaps queers are doing no better, as many of us also lie, cheat, and engage in no end of painful behavior. But the thing about heterosexual misery that makes it irreducible to basic human foible is that straight relationships are rigged from the start. Straight culture, unlike queer culture, naturalizes and often glorifies men's failures and women's suffering, hailing girls and women into heterofemininity through a collective performance of resilience. For instance, straight women's suffering, and men's redemption, played itself out on the national stage in 2016 with the release of Beyoncé's opus *Lemonade*, which chronicled Jay-Z's lying and infidelity and Beyoncé's rage and ultimate forgiveness. Here again, popular discourse seized on the opportunity to position a Black woman as an exemplar of heteroromantic survival. The Ethiopian American writer Hannah Giorgis, writing for the *Atlantic*, explains that very little was required of Jay-Z for him to be forgiven:

> Male redemption narratives have rarely required of their leading figures any meaningful restoration or atonement. The simple act of apologizing is enough to warrant a second act. Of course, Beyoncé is entitled to forgive her husband, . . . [but this] redemption tour is not simply a private burying of grievances, but also a public statement, a literal performance of absolution wrought through female suffering. [Their subsequent joint album] *Everything Is Love* . . . ends with Jay celebrating Bey—and the myriad other black women like her—by praising her ability to endure his misdeeds. . . . But the suggestion . . . that women's pain is the sole vehicle for male redemption, is exhausting. Who rescues the rescuer?[38]

Giorgis speaks, indirectly, to one of the primary reasons that straight culture remains unaddressed, or "unrescued" from itself: people cannot be rescued from forms of suffering that they themselves relate to as badges of honor.

## The Lack of Imagination

"I find straight culture to be too 'normal.' In other words, straight people are held to their own puritanical inhibitions with regards to sex, night life, and overall interactions with the broader public. . . . I find most mainstream straight people to be sad, repressed, and oblivious." (queer Latino cis male)

"Their relationships are limited and the roles between cis men and women are too traditional. . . . Straight cis men take up too much space." (queer Black woman)

"Maybe the worst part of straight culture/people is the limited imagination. I'm talking about straight, white, middle class American culture to be specific. . . . Now that I am in the queer community, I love my body, voice, hair, mind, etc." (queer white transmasculine dyke)

"Many hetero identified people see the world in black and white, . . . but I find that queer people are better able to see the black, white, shades of grey, AND colors too. Straight culture seems as foreign to me as learning to speak a new language." (queer Indigenous, Xican@ male)

"Mainly toxic masculinity . . . I also feel bad for straight people who feel so confined in their sexual identities that they feel stifled." (queer, Hispanic, Puerto Rican)

"Straight culture, I dunno. I don't think they really have a culture outside of the conformity and curious closets, like kink, mistresses, love children, secret abortions, etc." (queer African American woman)

"Their obsession with romantic love? I feel like queer people are more open to intimate friendships and since we often choose our family units, our friendships mean more. Straights are just completely obsessed with monogamy and gender roles." (queer white)

"The assumed normality of their lives. The preoccupation with my reproductive plans (I am child-free by choice and that's more than some can comprehend)." (queer African American lesbian)

"What makes me sad and what seems to be a hallmark of straight culture is the individual buy-in to the idea that women have no other options than settling for disappointing romantic/sexual/everything relationships. . . . It feels like your whole life path is scripted in straight culture. . . . I think I would feel so hopeless and sad and bored and unexcited and trapped. . . . It seems like straight culture grooms you to be a better tool of capitalism by accepting ways of living that are boring and exhausting without question." (queer femme, white, cis woman)

"They tend to have a limited imagination for formations of sexual and romantic relationships and base their own relationships on ownership." (queer Latinx, genderqueer)

"I think straight people's obsession with monogamy and the nuclear family unit makes people miserable. . . . If a partner does any sexual act with another person, in straight culture the relationship is automatically ruined with no possibility of reparation. Straight people get jealous, possessive, and I think all of these things make straight people miserable." (queer mixed, Mexican, Jewish woman)

Another standout feature of straight culture, in the eyes of many queers, is that it feels myopic and constrained, as if straight people are unable to see or understand all of the potentially liberatory sexual and gender options available to them. This stands in stark contrast with one of my favorite features of queer subculture: our love of elaborate sexual and gender typologies. Having come up as a queer dyke shaped by a convergence of lesbian feminist ethics, the HIV/AIDS movement, and queer kink/BDSM subculture, it seemed to me that the guiding sexual ethos of queer feminist life was to ask, How intimate, creative, debauched, and caretaking can we get with one another, what names can we give to these new forms of relating, and what rules do we need to put in place to make sure we enact them safely, sanely, and consensually? While the topic at hand is straight culture, we need to acknowledge this queer sexual ethos in order to contextualize some of the queer frustration described above about the smallness and scriptedness of straight life.

Queer efforts to stretch people's erotic imaginations and vocabularies are too numerous to list, but one of the most famous is the Handkerchief Code, a color-coded system for publicly displaying one's sexual preferences that was invented by gay and bi men in the 1970s. Instead of reducing desire to gender alone (e.g., "I'm a gay man, and you're a gay man, so having sex will probably work out just fine for us"), the Handkerchief Code was premised on the queer understanding that desire for particular sex acts, role play, or power statuses are equally important elements of sexual desire and compatibility. Different-colored handkerchiefs, worn in either one's right or left back pocket, signaled whether one wanted to be a top or bottom and what specific sex acts and role play one was interested in. In a similar vein, the lesbian feminist anthropologist Esther Newton wrote an essay in 1984 titled "The Misunderstanding: Toward a More Precise Sexual Vocabulary," in which she reflected on the time she had sex with her best friend, Shirley, an encounter they both found surprisingly unsatisfying despite being attracted to each other and finding the *idea* of sex with each other quite hot. After many conversations about why they ultimately had no erotic chemistry, they concluded that the missing element had nothing to do with gender or sexual orientation or body type. Instead, both of them like to be dominant during sex; both of them were tops. This realization inspired Newton to develop "a more precise sexual vocabulary" than the one available in straight culture, one that could help distinguish between gender preferences, one's own self-identity and expression, one's position within relations of power, and the nuts-and-bolts sex acts that one enjoys (Newton termed these "sexual preference," "erotic identity," "erotic role," and "erotic acts," respectively).[39] In yet another example, the lesbian theorist Kate Bornstein bemoaned in 1994 that "sexual orientation/preference is based in this culture solely on the gender of one's partner of choice," despite the fact that many other creative possibilities *could* be equally or more significant.[40] Bornstein offered a tantalizing list of other ways of classifying sexual desire, including a butch/femme-style model (in which attraction to femininity, for example, could include desire for feminine women and feminine men), a top/bottom model (in which people desire tops or bottoms or switches, regardless of gender), and a sex-acts model (in which people desire others who like anal sex, for instance).

Sometimes queer sexual typologies are not just about desire but about how to reimagine sexual partnerships so that they don't suffer from the cycle of possessive monogamy, lying, and infidelity that damages so many straight relationships. In a 1997 article called "Flexible Fidelity," the queer scholar D. Travers Scott laid out a system of ten different types of (non)monogamy that he and his partner, Dave, had imagined and explored, ranging from complete monogamy ("plus porn") to monogamy plus mutually-agreed-upon third parties to nonmonogamy only when out of town to nonmonogamy only with strangers (no friends or exes) and so on. Scott gave each of these options a fun name (for example, "boomerang = do whatever you want, but always come home"). Scott concluded, "Ultimately, your relationship can be as flexible, idiosyncratic, and unpredictable as your libido. . . . Being not-straight taught me that the old rules don't work. I'm interested in new, tailored versions . . . so [we] charted a map of possibilities."[41] As Scott indicated, the impetus for many of queer culture's best insights is the desire not to reproduce the failed practices of straight culture.

And, of course, in queer life, gender and sexual identities themselves continually proliferate, sometimes to the chagrin of straight people who complain about our swelling acronym. As many of my queer students will tell you, people are not simply straight, gay, or bisexual; we can also be pansexual, polysexual, monosexual, asexual, demisexual, graysexual, androsexual, gynesexual, skoliosexual, panromantic, demiromantic, and questioning/curious. This increasingly precise sexual vocabulary attempts to give a fuller picture of the variability of sexual desire—differences that straight culture renders unimaginable by refusing to give name to them.

The comments above about the lack of sexual (or even simply relational) imagination in straight culture resonate deeply for me, as straight people often seem to me either incapable of or uninterested in learning to think differently about gender and sexuality. Sometimes straight culture seems so totalizing, so hegemonic, that it can blind its adherents to all other possibilities. Thinking psychoanalytically about straightness, the French feminist philosopher Monique Wittig put it this way: "The straight mind cannot conceive of a culture, a society where heterosexuality would not order not only all human relationships but also its very production of concepts and all the processes which escape consciousness, as well."[42] Basically, straightness shapes everything, precisely by narrowing the field of what is conceivable or limiting the imagination. This is one of the reasons why the late queer theorist José Esteban Muñoz defined queerness not as a sexual orientation, per se, but as a utopian longing, a feeling of being pulled toward a queerer future, as yet unimagined.[43]

Of course, straight culture is now somewhat conscious of those elements of queer subculture that can be co-opted, especially when profitable. This slow drip of queer ideas in the straight mainstream accounts for one of the reasons that straight culture is experienced by queers as *boring*: straight culture can feel decades behind the curve (i.e., straight people are constantly "discovering" things, like conscious uncoupling or androgyny or *50 Shades of Grey*–style kink, et cetera, that dykes and fags spearheaded years ago). Relatedly, the feminist pornographer and sex educator Tristan Taormino once gave a guest lecture in one of my courses about the myriad ways that lesbians have mentored straight people about sex and relationships. We can thank lesbian feminists for the spate of well-lit, shame-free, and education-oriented sex shops (like Good Vibrations and Toys in Babeland) where average straight couples can now buy sex toys without feeling like deviants. We can thank lesbian feminists for the concept of ethical nonmonogamy, the existence of feminist porn, the bold notion that people can remain friends and family with ex-lovers, the emphasis on consent and care within kink practices, and the radical idea that women can strap on dildos and penetrate people, including their boyfriends and husbands. It is no wonder, then, that queer people feel sad about, and sometimes exhausted by, the "limited imagination" characteristic of straight culture. What straight people don't know *does* hurt them, and queer people often find themselves launching a rescue effort.

## Straight Rituals

"I find their flirtation rituals strange. Especially when I see a strong and independent woman get coy and cutesy around men." (queer, lesbian, Caucasian)

"The hysteria around straight weddings is very off-putting. . . . It feels very superficial with the pageantry of it all (even with all the events that lead up to it, for example, the engagement picture where the couple is in a random field/meadow/open land. Maybe it's symbolic?)." (queer multiracial Asian American woman)

"It's about taking off garters at weddings, and pink and blue cupcakes at gender reveal parties, and His and Her towels. Basically, it's not creative and I am too busy." (queer white FTM nonbinary dyke)

"I find that straight people have everyday rituals that require the participation of all people engaged around them. . . . I find there's a lot of conversation that leads to comparing amassed goods around the household that are coded in various ways. Questions about the latest home gadget, decorative accent pieces. I think to myself, why is this important? These conversations tend to evolve into who has 'better stuff.'" (genderqueer cis-passing man of color, Asian, Filipina/o/x)

"I find gender reveal parties absolutely bizarre. No one will ever convince me that it is normal or healthy to celebrate the biological genitalia of an unborn baby. That's weird." (queer, nonbinary, Caucasian)

"Baby gender reveal parties. Hating your wife. Straight men refusing to do household chores, or worse, expecting to be congratulated for having done even the smallest amount." (queer, white cis fem)

Being a queer person compelled to participate in straight rituals can be an alienating and cringe-worthy experience. This has happened to me countless times, but one memorably uncomfortable example was when I was hired at UC Riverside and was the only queer faculty member in my department. Several of my older colleagues lived in McMansions in gated communities, wore Dockers, and liked to host poolside department parties at their homes during which they would stand around in heterosexual married couplets, drinking white wine and talking about sports cars, the successes of their grown children, or whether to buy a boat. My whiteness and recent university degree marked me as someone who would be welcomed into this life, but it was not a life that could recognize me or one I wanted anything to do with. I was thirty-one years old and lived far away from campus in a tiny apartment in a dyke enclave with my punk trans partner. I spent my weekends dancing in a naughty queer femme burlesque troupe. I was out to my colleagues as a lesbian, but I was not out to them as a radical queer for fear that I would make them uncomfortable and damage my chances at tenure (I would later move to UCR's Department of Gender and Sexuality Studies, resolving this dilemma). The point here is that I spent those first several years in my job witnessing, celebrating, and participating in straight rituals without any of my colleagues even noticing the emotional labor this required.

One could argue that all rituals can be strange or tedious to outsiders, and of course queer people have our own rituals, many of them now clichéd. I don't know a single queer person who has hosted a baby-gender-reveal party or a bridal shower, but I *have* been to a couple of queer weddings that I found alienating and boring. I also find coming-out stories, like detailed descriptions of other people's dreams, to be therapeutic for the teller but mostly uninteresting and platitudinous for the listener. Drag-queen performances and dyke psychosexual dramas are other queer traditions I enjoyed when I was younger but now find so predictable that I can hardly bear them.

These issues aside, the above comments from my respondents point to the fact that straight rituals are oppressive on a far greater order of magnitude, because of not only their disturbing content (e.g., throwing a party to announce the shape of an unborn baby's genitals) but also their *compulsory* force. Heteronormativity is not a neutral cultural formation organized around a natural, freely occurring sexual preference but an obligatory system structuring many of the world's societies, a system "that has had to be imposed, managed, organized, propagandized and maintained by force."[44] As one comrade explains above, straight rituals feel like they "require the participation of all [people] engaged around them," including queer people. This is because heteronormative rituals—coming-of-age parties, engagement parties, bridal showers, bachelor/ette parties, weddings, gender-reveal parties, baby showers, elaborately gendered children's birthday parties, Valentine's Day, anniversary parties—are the accepted traditions offered to all of us to celebrate passage through life. Heteronormative rituals shape how we understand the difference between youth and adulthood, success and failure, loneliness and connectedness. In straight culture, if women don't get married and have children and figure out how to stay attractive and keep their man, a cascade of tragic temporal consequences ensues: the clock is ticking, the window is closing, youthful beauty is fading, expensive interventions are needed. By contrast, while many of these heteronormative demands try to push their creepy tendrils into lesbian feminist culture, there remains considerable room for a feminist dyke to assert her disinterest in having children as a point of queer pride ("No breeders!") and to experience deep love and connection through intimate feminist friendships. This is not to mention my favorite aspect of aging in dyke subculture, which is that many ways of being (swagger, fierceness, sexual skills, good politics, intelligence, artistry, interest in particular kinks) are far more important than are youth and other glorified hetero body aesthetics. A dyke can be chubby, silver-haired, wizened, and sloppily dressed and still have *a lot* of game.

But straight culture is so hegemonic, so overdetermining, that it is often challenging to imagine how to have certain experiences in queer ways or without the imposition of heteronormative meaning. For instance, I have known a few dykes and nonbinary queers who decided not to get pregnant, despite some interest, because they sensed they would be unable to escape straight culture's rigidly hetero-gendered conceptualization of the pregnant body. The association of pregnancy with heterosexual reproduction and essential womanhood is changing, but the transformation is slow. Access to an experience like pregnancy requires that one be prepared to be hailed by straight culture; or, as Wittig states, "discourses of heterosexuality oppress us in the sense that they prevent us from speaking unless we speak in their terms."[45] I, too, have had difficulty speaking to straight people in my own terms, not theirs. When I was pregnant and straight women shared with me their ideas about, say, the differences between girl infants and boy infants, I weighed the benefit of being authentic against the risk of sounding like a jerk. The truth was that I did not share their perceptions of infant behavior and that I planned to parent differently than they had, to parent queerly. Sometimes I tried to explain what this meant to me, but I was often met with expressions of defensiveness or bafflement.

I have also struggled to explain to straight people what it means for an environment to *feel straight*, which is not simply about the presence or absence of gay people. A couple of years ago, my partner and I attended a banquet fund-raiser for our child's school—a school where the executive director is an out lesbian and almost all parents seem to us like gay-friendly liberals. As soon as we left the banquet, we turned to each other in the car and said, "Oh my god, was that one of the *straightest* events you have ever been to in your whole life?!" It was so validating to discover that we both felt that way, but at the time, neither of us was quite sure what it was that was *so straight*. Later I pieced together all of the straight rituals I observed that night, which had combined to create an intense experience of hetero immersion: women complaining about their husbands, middle-aged couples chatting about how the school fund-raiser was their big night out that year, men making bad jokes to which women responded with halfhearted laughter, women in the bathroom trading information about diet and exercise, donors to the school being referred to by their shared last name ("let's all thank the Petersons for their generous gift!"), the presence of many men I had never seen before because this is the only school event they show up for, "his" and "her" silent auction items, and more examples I can't recall. My partner and I, a genderqueer butch and a femme dyke, were welcome *at* the event, but the event was not *for* us.

## Obliviousness and the Straight Gaze

"Unexamined power and privilege; oblivious to perks they receive and operate out of; assumptions and assertions about gender roles; how they co-opt queer struggles, queer spaces, queer victories and take them as their own (love wins!), how they don't get on the front lines. Sometimes I feel enraged, often, I feel unsurprised and protect myself before I even know I am doing that." (queer South Asian, Indian, genderqueer)

"I sometimes feel like I am a zoo animal to them. They love to watch and observe but don't care outside of that." (queer Latino, biracial male)

"Most annoying of all might be the belief that all bisexual women are interested in having threesomes with heterosexual couples—I have so many straight people on dating apps who message me because they think I want to fuck them and their GF/BF/spouse. The last thing I want to be is somebody's sexual unicorn fantasy plaything. Black women get fetishized too much as it is." (queer mixed-race, Black and white, cis woman)

"Straight people can't seem to not talk about their sexuality or mine for more than 15 minutes at a time. I wish they'd just read more or just be queer since they seem so curious about it." (queer Black femme cis woman)

"The 'you're so brave and amazing for just being who you are' kind of comments feel patronizing and hard." (queer, white, genderqueer)

"Straight people can be way too familiar. I am in a 21-yr relationship and have been asked if I am the top or bottom, . . . unbelievably inappropriate." (queer Latino/Chicano male)

We can hardly blame straight people, and straight women in particular, for being interested in what's happening in queer spaces. Queer spaces are often a delicious mix of pleasure and danger; they can be bacchanalian, performative, and unpredictable, while also—owing to the general absence of straight men—being relatively safe environments for women. When a bevy of straight women looking for a good time decide to go to a gay bar—a phenomenon that has rankled some gay men and gained the attention of many a journalist[46]—they do this, understandably, to experience an exuberant and erotically charged environment without enduring the sexual harassment of straight men. But, ironically, a good number of straight women have ended up sexually harassing gay men during their excursions to the gay bar: they ogle and touch gay men's bodies without permission, they assume an automatic affinity between themselves and gay men, they "let loose" by engaging in drunken and disruptive behavior that centers themselves in a queer space, and they seem to be utterly oblivious to the effect of their presence. Writing about the popularity of gay bars as destination spots for straight women's bachelorette parties, the drag queen Miz Cracker describes how the bachelorette phenomenon has enabled the straight gaze to infiltrate precisely the spaces intended to be free of it:

[Straight women] run roughshod over the nerves of a gay room with their uncomfortable pronouncements and personal comments. *I'm, like, an honorary gay. I'm a gay man in a woman's body. Yes, queen, I live for your shoes! Ugh, why do gay guys have the best bodies? If you were straight, I would totally make out with you.* And so on. They declare their allegiance to queers, they make jokes based on outmoded perceptions of queer life—but most of all they make a lot of tone-deaf noise that can entirely ruin the night for a room full of queer patrons.[47]

This combination of self-absorption and the straight gaze—viewing queer people and places as novelties to be consumed—is yet another hallmark of straight culture, one encouraged by media representations of gay men as possessing special skills that they are just waiting to share with straight people—a sense of style, campy humor, a natural empathy for women, and so on. The TV series *Queer Eye* is the exemplar, featuring a team of fabulous queer men who provide deep listening and style advice to (mostly straight) makeover recipients.

But the story about how the straight gaze figures queer women is a different one, one in which lesbians and bisexual women play a central role in straight people's homosexual curiosities and their fantasies about threesomes. Like the respondent above, I have been asked for sex by straight people multiple times, mostly in queer bars where I was caught off guard by the presence of lascivious straight couples (who let these people in here?!). I want to note, too, that there is a distinct unevenness in the way straight women and straight men consume queer life, and most likely due to sexism, the media tend to focus on the irritating behaviors of straight women (who are easy targets) more than the threatening and violent behavior of straight men. While a bachelorette's invasion of a gay bar is certainly an annoying display of privilege, a straight man's invasion of a lesbian bar is *frightening*. On some of the occasions in which intoxicated straight men have tried to coax me into a threesome, I was not just aggravated; I was worried I might be raped.

Also illuminated in the comments above is the fact that even well-intentioned gestures of alliance can feel, to queer people, like further subjection to the straight gaze. It is not that queer people necessarily disagree with proclamations like "love is love" or with the idea that queer people are brave and beautiful. It is that these are platitudes that obscure queer complexities: Love is not exactly the point of queer liberation. Not all queer people want to be beautiful or brave. Telling us we're beautiful is telling us something we already know. Why do you think we care what you think to begin with? And the list of internal objections goes on. These kinds of statements—perhaps akin to "I don't see color"—have become such predictable staples of gay-friendly heterosexuality that their very utterance has become a beacon of *straight culture*.

## Bad Sex, Genital Obsession

"It's also really upsetting how few orgasms straight women have. . . . You deserve better, girl." (queer Latina)

"Their sex lives are really boring and dishonest. They'll 'spice things up' by using fuzzy handcuffs and think that it's wild. . . . I don't think that straight people are generally very good at exploring their sexuality or communicating their sexual desires to their partner. It seems sad and boring." (queer cis male, white)

"I find it strange how someone can not like someone based on their genitals. Being pansexual, the concept of someone being ruled out of partner status because of what their genitals are just is absurd to my mind." (gender fluid, Hispanic Latino)

"Actually, another article went around on Facebook among my straight friends too—this one about 'how men know when sex is over.' Every. Single. Man. Said 'when I cum.' . . . As a lesbian, I can't imagine stopping sex with my partner the minute I cum. It's kind of hilarious to think about!

. . . But of course it's also sad that this is apparently the reality for straight women." (queer white female)

The queer feminist scholar Angela Jones begins her essay "#Demand-BetterStraightSex!" with an experience that a straight woman friend once shared with her. Her friend described sex with her boyfriend, but she was also describing what is now a familiar story about straight sex: he thrusts, he's into it, he cums, she's barely present and is thinking about doing the laundry, he gets up, and it's over. Angela's friend seems confused: "Sometimes it just feels like he's raping me. I know he loves me, but why does he have to have sex with me when he knows I don't want to?"[48] Feminist research indicates that unwanted sex inside heterosexual relationships is so common and normalized that it a core part of the scaffolding of rape culture; there's a thin line between unwanted sex (the kind that many women have with husbands and boyfriends all the time) and sexual assault.[49] The #metoo movement—begun in 2006 by the antiviolence activist Tarana Burke—has also helped reveal the ubiquity of straight men's sexual violations of women. Numerous high-profile and well-loved men have raped women, drugged women, exposed their naked bodies to women, and masturbated in front of women without women's consent and with impunity. By 2017, the tidal wave of these stories was enough to make even the most jaded lesbian feminist ask herself again, *What the fuck is wrong with men?* and *How and why are straight women surviving heterosexuality?* You deserve better, girl.

Jones concludes that the answers to these questions are multiple and intersecting. Coercive and male-centric straight sex is normalized because heterosexual love is already constructed as a sacrifice for women, a point that is a central theme in this book. Beyond this, patriarchal power arrangements ensure that many straight women have few choices but to endure men's violence, as illuminated with gut-wrenching clarity in the 2019 documentary series *Lorena*, about both the long-standing sexual torture that Lorena Bobbitt endured at the hands of her husband and the misogynistic ridicule she experienced at the hands of the public. Men also pursue masculine validation through sexual dominance, Jones explains, thereby benefiting from a system that rewards straight men for dissociating from women's experience of sex. But an even more basic problem is that straight people define "actual sex" as penetration of a vagina by a penis, even though few women (about 18 percent) experience orgasm from this activity alone.[50] This accounts for the fact that 86 percent of lesbians report usually or always having orgasms during sex, compared to 65 percent of straight women.[51] Lesbians know that "sex" is hardly reducible to penetration, but more importantly, lesbians wear their capacity to make women cum as a badge of honor—a celebrated accomplishment within lesbian subculture.[52]

A secret about lesbian sex that I don't think I have ever seen written about before is that lesbians appreciate different things about the vulva and vagina than do straight men. If popular culture and the rise of vaginal tightening and rejuvenation procedures are any indication, straight men value a "tight" vagina. But this is incomprehensible to me as a dyke. If I only had a nickel for every time I have heard queer people brag about being size queens with capacious vaginas and/or anuses that welcome fists and giant dildos, I'd be a rich woman! In queer space, what makes an orifice "good" is not how it feels to the person going inside it (for whom it might make sense for the emphasis to be on tightness) but how the orifice feels about itself: what it wants, what it can do, what it can enjoy. For many humans, the capacity to take something *very large* into one's body is extremely pleasurable, and this is much more difficult when one has been told that the goal is to keep all orifices small and tight. It is fine, of course, if size is not one's thing, but the point here is that it makes queer people—like my comrades quoted above—quite sad that in straight culture, a vagina is evaluated according to its capacity to please men and not its capacity to experience pleasure.[53]

Another troubling feature of straight culture's relationship to sex is its obsession with gendered body parts: the genitals of fetuses (*you're invited to our gender-reveal party!*), the inherent homosexuality of men's anuses (*even though it is my wife's finger in my butt, something about it still feels gay*), the genitals of trans people (*but who are you, really?!*), and so on. In addition to the creative ways that queer people have decoupled sex from gender, and gender from sexuality, perhaps the fact that queer people have a less genital-to-genital understanding of sex (queer sex also looks like mouths to genitals and anuses, sex toys to genitals and anuses) also helps account for the fact that many queer people are pansexual, capable of intimacy and attraction to people regardless of their bodies or gender identities.

## The Goodness in Straight People

"I don't find straight people or culture to be sad or off-putting, . . . but then again, some of the straight people I know are really just discovering their queerness and are beginning to open up to the possibilities. Sexuality is such a fluid thing. . . . I have always felt that way. For example, I remember when you were straight, Jane. I never thought of you as sad or off putting. . . . I always thought you were amazing to hang out with. And I remember when I was straight identified. . . . I think I was just as awesome then. . . . Being queer didn't make me any better." (genderqueer woman, Palestinian born, raised in United States)

And lastly, this chapter comes to a close by acknowledging that, of course, straight people are not reducible to straight culture. Many straight people relate to their heterosexuality in dazzlingly feminist and queer ways. Many straight people, including straight men, are lovable, vulnerable humans. And many straight people have queer futures ahead of them, like I once had. I love the person quoted above, who brings us back to the goodness in straight people, though it does not escape me that their two examples—myself and themselves—are people who would later identify as queer. What does it mean that "queering heterosexuality" is often offered as the best route forward for straight people to achieve some degree of gender and sexual justice? Is it possible that heterosexuality, qua heterosexuality, can rescue itself from its own tragic condition? These are the questions at the heart of chapter 5.

# 5

# DEEP HETEROSEXUALITY

## Toward a Future in Which Straight Men Like Women So Much That They Actually Like Women

I WROTE THIS BOOK OUT OF SOLIDARITY WITH STRAIGHT women, but the further into the project I went, the more my attention shifted to straight men. Straight men have caused women unthinkable suffering, and yet I share with them, presumably, something that has been fundamental and significant in my life—a desire to partner with women. In this chapter, I speak mostly to straight men about how they might be even straighter than they are, if by "straightness" we mean an orientation toward women. I implore them to put their politics where their lust is: in alignment with women. I call upon the wisdom of the dyke experience to illuminate for straight men the human capacity to desire, to fuck, and to be feminist comrades at the same time. Once again, I return to the insights of lesbian feminism, in this case to map the ways that lust for women, and deep regard for women, have lived in complementary relationship to each other.

My reflections on the possibilities for heterosexuality build on, but also depart from, writing centered on the project of queering straightness. Queer observers of the heterosexual miseries detailed in this book have often speculated that the most direct path toward the subversion of straight culture is for straight people to be more honest about their perverse desires and gender-bending curiosities (think about all those straight men waiting for Halloween, their one socially sanctioned opportunity to dress in drag). Gender scholars have wondered, for instance, whether heterosexuals could be kinky enough—by, let's say, having a sexual dynamic anchored in men's submission and women's dominance or by being participants in BDSM communities in which gendered and racialized power and consent are explicit and ongoing topics of conversation—that their perversion poses a challenge to heteropatriarchy and white supremacy.[1] Other queers have ruminated on whether polyamory, which requires a less possessive and nonnuclear approach to sexual relationships as well as a commitment to transparency about desire and jealousy, could pierce through some of straight men's sense of entitlement to, and ownership of, women.[2] Some have hypothesized that gender-subversive sex acts themselves, like "pegging" (women's anal penetration of men), could be a backdoor route to undermining men's patriarchal authority by redefining heteromasculinity as receptive and vulnerable.[3] In my teaching, I have shared all of these examples with my students, offering them as ways that some straight people transgress the bounds of heteronormativity. And yet I continue to be concerned about their practical applications for the vast majority of ordinary straight people (i.e., my intuition tells me that some of my straight relatives and neighbors are not quite ready for BDSM or polyamory—perhaps pegging . . . ?).

Some queer commentators have focused less on how straight people's *sex* practices might be queered and more on how straight people might shake up their broader life choices by, for example, refusing marriage or child-centeredness or valuing friendships and chosen family as much as or more than blood connections. For instance, Jack Halberstam has argued for a queer form of feminism, a "gaga feminism," in which straight people embrace the postmodern instability of traditional heterosexuality and let the impending queerness of the future wash over them.[4] Among the queer transformations that Halberstam believes have the potential to reshape heterosexuality are reproductive technologies that enable late-in-life pregnancies and "pregnant men," disillusioned and heteroflexible straight women who divorce their husbands in their forties in favor of more satisfying queer relationships, and the rise in solo parenting and awareness of the doubtful value of fathers. While feminist projects have long aspired to transform and enlist straight men into the movement for gender equality, Halberstam's vision seems to leave straight men, deemed basically hopeless, on the cutting-room floor. In this version of straight women's lives, men play only a small role.

These are promising approaches, and there is no doubt that the gravity of the tragedy of heterosexuality requires a wide array of tactics. And yet my years of teaching and writing about heterosexuality have led me to rethink whether offering queerness to straight people, where queerness is defined as practices of gender and sexual nonnormativity, is the most practical or empathic way of attending to the daily injustices of straight women's lives or to the material and cultural realities of heterosexual desire. Some straight women I know are structurally bound up in relationships with men that produce resentment but also security and comfort, disadvantage but also privilege. The privileges associated with heterosexuality are amplified for women of color and poor and working-class women, for whom other sources of power are unavailable. Moreover, "straightness" as an embodied desire for the opposite sex is, for many straight people, inseparable from a desire for gender and/or sexual respectability and cultural legibility.[5] Straight people can be very attached to being straight, both erotically and culturally.

In light of all of these complexities, I want to come at straightness with an interest in actualization, rather than undoing. As detailed in chapter 2, the conditions of patriarchy have long damaged men's desire for women, and women's for men, such that heterosexuality, as a sexual orientation, was always already a contradiction. Women were too inferior, too degraded, for men to actually *like*. Women could be sexually desired, and they could be paternalistically loved; but they could not be engaged as autonomous, self-determining humans in the way that men related to other men. Consequently, much of men's energy was directed toward men and not women; this includes erotic energy, if we understand the erotic as it was defined by the late Black lesbian feminist Lorde. For Lorde, "the erotic" is a kind of power that arises from knowing one's own capacity for joy and pleasure, as well as in the encounter between people who can share that self-knowing pleasure with one another. Lorde explained that one of patriarchy's tools is to deny women this power, to offer it to us in only superficial forms "in order to exercise it in the service of men."[6] Straight men, on the other hand, have created countless rituals, games, art forms, traditions, and spaces designed to explore and pursue their own pleasure, typically in the company of other men. The formation of modern heteromasculinity is marked by erotic competition among men for women's bodies, public conquest of women's bodies as a spectacle for other men, and the construction of sex itself as an act of men's collective force or manipulation, women's collective gift or sacrifice, and a cultural encounter in which men's pleasure is the driving impulse, the inevitable focal point.[7] In other words, straight men have spent an inordinate amount of time exchanging erotic power and forging erotic bonds with *one another* but have struggled to interest themselves with women's sexual pleasure and consent. It is no wonder, then, that one source of queer alienation from straight culture is that heterosexuality often rings false; straight men do not actually like the very people they have claimed as their object of desire and affection. Straight men do not need to be queered; they need to learn to like women.

## Deep Heterosexuality

Rather than pushing heterosexuality in queerer directions, what if we honored its basic impulses—that is, women's and men's desire and/or love for each other—but urged this impulse to go deeper, to reconcile its contradictions? How might the heterosexual impulse be taken to its most humane and fulfilling, and least violent and disappointing, conclusion? Is it not possible that women and men could feel an attraction to each other that was so unstoppable, so expansive, so hungry for the wholeness of the other that it forged strong bonds of *identification and deep mutual regard*, rather than oppositeness and hierarchy?

In evoking "deep heterosexuality," I borrow from the queer feminist artist Allyson Mitchell, whose project "Deep Lez" weaves together the old and the new, the most useful theories and practices from the rich archive of lesbian feminist herstory with contemporary intersectional, transfeminist politics. Deep Lez allows us to mine what is liberatory about the practice of women loving women, without dismissing this herstory outright for its essentialism, false universalism, or other limitations.[8]

Similarly, I imagine deep heterosexuality as a framework for honoring and preserving what straight people experience as fulfilling about hetero sex and straight culture and for pushing further and deeper in these pleasurable hetero directions. Deep heterosexuality turns to the erotic, the hetero erotic, as a potential source of connection and mutual regard built through the channels of desire, joy, and pleasure. Deep heterosexuality proclaims: if straight women and men are actually attracted to each other, that is excellent. Now let's expand the notion of heterosexual attraction to include such a powerful longing for the full humanity of women, and for the sexual vulnerability of men, that anything less becomes suspect as authentic heterosexual desire. Deep heterosexuality draws on lesbian feminist insights about the nexus of desire and identification in order to help release straight people from the binds of a sexual orientation characterized by attraction to people one dislikes.[9] Deep heterosexuality accesses the erotic as a site of identification, mutual recognition, and joy, and when this happens, as Audre Lorde explains, "we begin to give up, of necessity, being satisfied with suffering and self-negation, and with the numbness which so often seems like their only alternative in our society."[10]

The most useful model I have found for how to like women, and to fuck women feministly, comes from lesbian feminists. For the remainder of this chapter, I look closely at two lesbian feminist interventions from which we can draw insights relevant to the project of deep heterosexuality. The first is a uniquely lesbian feminist approach to denaturalizing heterosexuality, which I believe is an essential first step toward bringing deep heterosexuality into its fullest expression. The second is a set of lesbian feminist instructions, or examples, for how to identify with someone and fuck them at the same time (i.e., how to desire women humanely). I offer these gifts to straight men.

## Accountability: Choosing to Be Straight

One of the foundational principles of lesbian feminism is that each person's sexual desire is their own responsibility, if not something they can choose, then at least something they can choose to examine and take ownership of. Two decades before the emergence of what we now call queer theory, lesbian feminists argued for a vision of sexuality as a site of choice and political resistance. A far cry from today's "born this way" approach to sexual orientation, which has been most widely embraced by gay men, lesbian feminists claimed their love of women as a cultivated political stance, an act of opposition to heteropatriarchy. As the lesbian poet Cheryl Clarke explained in 1983, one might call oneself a lesbian not only, or even primarily, because of a sexual attraction to women's bodies but for a host of other political, cultural, psychological, and spiritual reasons: "I name myself 'lesbian' because I want to be visible to other black lesbians. I name myself 'lesbian' because I do not subscribe to predatory/institutionalized heterosexuality. I name myself lesbian because I want to be with women (and they don't all have to call themselves 'lesbians'). I name myself 'lesbian' because it is part of my vision. I name myself lesbian because being woman-identified has kept me sane. I call myself 'Black,' too, because Black is my perspective, my aesthetic, my politics, my vision, my sanity."[11] Borrowing from this rich lesbian feminist tradition of taking responsibility for one's desire and articulating what it accomplishes in the broader context of one's life, deep heterosexuality invites straight people to also develop accountability for their sexual orientation, or to decide to own their straightness. If, like Cheryl Clarke, straight women and men were to develop a list of reasons that they have named themselves "straight," what would be on this list? If we abandoned all pretense that heterosexuality is the only option, or that it is easy, simple, automatic, predetermined, and not worth talking and thinking about, how might straight women and men articulate what propels them toward each other, despite all the difficulty? Though we are all socialized under the force of heteronormativity, not all of us are straight. But those who are could learn to relate to their heterosexuality as a cultivated desire of which they are agent, rather than victim or passive recipient.

This kind of reframe is, I believe, especially crucial for straight men, who have been encouraged to relate to their desire for women as so physiological as to be outside of their control and so compartmentalized as to enable the disconnect between wanting women and liking them. This very narrow and conditional way that men have learned to desire women is arguably a fraction of what that desire *could* entail, making heteromasculinity a strikingly feeble and impotent mode of attraction to women compared with what is possible for dykes and other women-desiring queers. As the Radicalesbians articulated it, women who desire other women provide their counterparts not only with sex but also with "personhood," "a revolutionary force," "freedom," "mirroring," "solidarity," "emotional support," "the melting of barriers," and "real-ness."[12] I am not suggesting that sex should always reach such a high bar but instead pointing out how revealing it is that when straight boys or men describe a similarly comprehensive interest in the lives of girls or women (say, perhaps, they are so attracted to women that they are interested in books or movies about women, women's art, women's emotional lives), they risk being perceived as a bit "gay." Transforming straight men's fragile and damaged desire for women into something robust, convincing, and worth all that braggadocio requires that men are willing to actively cultivate and strengthen their heterosexuality, their desire for women, rather than expecting nature to handle things—that strategy has clearly not worked. Rather than feeling victimized by women (and deriding women partners as people who "control sex," who are the old ball and chain, who talk too much, and so on), straight men could recognize that heterosexuality is the path they have chosen, or at least it is the path that they are on, and that this path is about being "oriented" toward women. That is its very definition!

The increasing popularity of biological accounts of sexual orientation is one of the latest obstacles to deep heterosexuality. When people believe heterosexuality is natural and hardwired, and when they have never known a heterosexuality free from some degree of patriarchal suffering, then this suffering also seems natural, even inevitable.[13] If straight people are born straight and cannot change the fact of their straightness, and if patriarchy is a powerful, enduring system that is painfully slow to change and also inextricably tied to heterosexuality, then what is left for straight people to feel except some mix of resignation and cruel optimism? Indeed, this is what straight feminist women often *do* seem to feel; they feel that the problem runs so deep that it is unlikely to be resolved in their own lifetimes.

Through a queer lens, heteroresignation or heteropessimism appears to be a rite of passage for straight women.[14] As much gets conveyed in a meme-worthy scene from the sitcom *Parks and Recreation*, in which best friends Ann Perkins and Leslie Knope (played by Rashida Jones and Amy Poehler) are asked if they are a couple, to which Knope lightheartedly retorts, "No, tragically, we are both heterosexual." Poehler's character acknowledges heterosexuality as "tragic," but the scene remains cheery because this acknowledgment is so familiar within women's culture as to be taken for granted, almost cute. It poses no existential crisis for these characters to describe their sexual orientation as tragic, nor is it implied that something should or could be done to address the tragedy. On social media, a screenshot of the scene went viral, with straight women tagging their women friends—the ones who inhabit a similar (pseudowife) position in their own lives.

We know that straight culture likes to glorify itself, but it also, paradoxically, frames straight women as hapless victims of their sexual orientation. Are they? Many lesbian feminists certainly believed this (hence the call for straight women to leave men and become "political

**Figure 5.1.** Heterosexuality is tragic. (From *Parks and Recreation*)

lesbians"). Adrienne Rich famously argued in 1980 that heterosexuality was imposed on women, and therefore women could not experience freedom even in seemingly healthy heterosexual relationships: "The question inevitably will arise: Are we then to condemn all heterosexual relationships, including those that are least oppressive? I believe this question, though often heartfelt, is the wrong question here. . . . The absence of [women's] choice remains the great unacknowledged reality, and in the absence of choice, women will remain dependent on the chance or luck of particular relationships and will have no collective power to determine the meaning and place of sexuality in their lives."[15] But most straight feminist women with whom I have spoken about this subject do not view themselves as having been manipulated or forced into being straight. And even if they did, straight-identified women's ability to imagine that they have no choice but to partner with men is arguably challenged by the growing public visibility of bisexual and lesbian relationships.

Heteronormativity nonetheless erases the need for straight people to justify or explain their sexuality, to others and to themselves: What does being straight do for them? What do they like about it? When did they first know they were straight? When I ask straight feminist women such questions—including "Why are you straight?" and "What do you like about men?"—I am struck by how often they look like deer caught in headlights. Some feminist women suggest that there is not much they like about straightness other than sexual encounters with men. They believe straightness is a bad deal for women, and yet they feel a physical attraction to men that they don't feel for women. My reaction to that is, if it is true that desire for sex with men is powerful enough for some women that it makes heterosexuality more desirable than queerness or asexuality, then this is itself an amazing fact—one that intervenes in the oft-cited notion that women care more about emotional connection than they do about sex. For straight feminist women, even this assertion—"I am in it for the dick," as one straight friend told me—is an important first step toward deromanticizing women's gendered suffering and exposing the cost-benefit analysis that is part of any heterosexual encounter under patriarchy. In other cases, women may not be in it for men's bodies at all but for the respectability or security that heterosexuality offers. This, too, is a powerful truth for women to own, as it exposes the transactional bind in which straight women are still positioned after centuries of servitude and exploitation. Ideally, women are in it for pleasure—in which I would include the concept of love and also the dick and even the social benefits of heterosexuality. But again, if heterosexuality were a site of significant pleasure for women, this raises questions about why so many straight women appear to be miserable. For straight women, the work at hand is to cultivate some kind of agentic relationship to the fact that they have not chosen queerness.

Straight men have already made it loud and clear that many of them are in it for the sex and free labor, so their work is not to acknowledge this but to recognize it as an utterly incomplete mode of desiring women—a feeble version of what heterosexuality could be. For straight women and men, accountability means piercing through the fantasy we're all sold about the natural ease and happiness of heterosexuality and instead learning to recognize the structural and cultural conditions that have produced, but also stunted, their heterosexuality.

## Liking Women, or, Women-Identified Men

A basic premise of straight culture is the idea that gendered bodies, especially women's bodies, require purification and modification to be desirable—shaving, perfuming, toning, refining, shrinking, enlarging, and antiaging. But in queer spaces, it is often precisely the hairy, sweaty, dirty, smelly, or unkempt gendered body that is most beloved. I recall the first time I entered a gay men's sex shop, in the 1990s in the Castro district of San Francisco, and encountered a barrel full of lightly stained and dingy-looking "used jock straps" for sale. It was my introduction to the fact that there were people in the world who desired men's bodies so much that they wanted deep, intimate, and seemingly unconditional contact with them—even and especially the parts of men's bodies that straight women seemed to want to avoid. Most straight women I knew, no doubt due to their socialization as girls and women, appreciated men's bodies for their sexual functionality but not as a site of objectification that they were excited to dive into and explore—to smell, taste, or penetrate.[16] Similarly, I have been to dozens of dyke strip shows, burlesque shows, drag-king shows, and sex shows in which women's armpit hair and leg hair and facial hair or their body fat or their genderqueer bodies have been precisely the objects of the audience's collective lust. Fat bodies and hairy bodies are also staples of queer dyke porn, not relegated to a fetish category. In other words, queer desire is marked by a lustful appreciation for even those parts of men's and women's bodies that have been degraded by straight culture. Like a food adventurer who delights in those parts of the animal or plant deemed undesirable by the narrowing of mainstream tastes, queer people's desire for the full animal has been less constrained. Recognizing this suggests that gay men may have a deeper or more comprehensive appreciation for men's bodies than do straight women, just as lesbians' lust for women is arguably more expansive and forgiving than straight men's.

But most importantly, because queer circuits of desire do not rely on the erotic encounter of "opposites" embedded in a broader culture of gendered acrimony and alienation, queer lust need not reconcile a conflict between wanting to fuck and generally disliking one's fuckable population. Queer desire does not immediately hit up against prescripted, institutionally sanctioned misogyny. This means that something very powerful is possible in queer life that I rarely see in straight culture: a merging of objectifying desire, on the one hand, and a feminist, subjectifying respect for those who are desired, on the other. In sex-positive queer feminist subculture, for instance, lust for women's bodies is sometimes delightfully lewd and lascivious but not at the expense of women's subjectivity. One of the many significant legacies of lesbian feminism is that its vision of "loving women" integrated the libidinous and the subjectifying.

I want to consider whether it is possible to extend to straight men this lesbian feminist mode of desire. Granted, many of the thinkers to whom I now turn believed that heterosexuality was unsalvageable and incongruous with feminism, but they nonetheless created a vision for devotion to women that is expansive enough, I believe, to be of use to people of all genders who want to like women, including straight men. For instance, being "woman identified" was a core element of lesbian feminist practice, and while it often referred to women's *self*-identification, or learning to love the self through intimacy with other women, it also referred to the practice of investing in women's collective freedom and self-determination. Lesbian feminist ethics dictated that to lust after women, to want to fuck women—even casually or nonmonogamously or raunchily—was inseparable from being *identified* with women as a whole and with the project of wanting women's freedom. It meant learning about what lifted women up, and also what harmed them, and aligning one's desires in the direction of women's collective liberation rather than their suffering. For example, it looked like what Adrienne Rich called "marriage resistance," or the recognition that marriage and nuclear family arrangements typically benefited men but disadvantaged women. Therefore, Rich argued, to have genuine regard for women logically meant not attempting to own them in marriage or otherwise block their intimacy with friends and comrades or inhibit their capacity to live engaged and meaningful lives. For the Radicalesbians, to desire women meant that one's "energies flowed toward women," that one desired to "relate more completely to women."[17] It meant disinvesting in "male identification," or in the practice of supporting, benefiting from, justifying, and being complicit with patriarchal interests. It meant recognizing that while straight men claimed to love women, in fact their energies flowed toward men— toward admiring men, seeking men's approval, forging bonds with men, and so on. Heterosexuality, lesbian feminists recognized, was an oppressively homosocial—and often homoerotic—institution that romanticized men and women's alienation from each other.

At the time of the nascent lesbian feminist movement, it was scarcely imaginable that straight men might themselves be capable of woman identification, and hence deep heterosexuality was largely unthinkable. Heterosexuality relied not only on a gender dichotomy that positioned men and women as opposites types incapable of identification with each other but also on a subject/object erotic model in which desire could only be forged and sustained through degrees of difference, distance, and mystery. In 1992, the straight feminist writer Naomi Wolf reproduced this notion when she described, in *Ms.* magazine, a new mode of straightness that she called "radical heterosexuality." Radical heterosexuality, according to Wolf, had roughly six goals: (1) straight women needed to be financially independent and/or have the skills necessary to leave an abusive relationship; (2) legal marriage needed to be abolished in favor of something akin to (then illegal) gay and lesbian commitment rituals and "chosen family"; (3) straight men needed to disavow patriarchal privilege; (4) straight women needed to disavow the privileges associated with femininity; (5) radical heterosexuals needed to resist their "gender imprinting," or their erotic investment in traditional gender roles; and, relatedly, (6) feminists needed to forgive one another for their attachments to the gender binary given that gender roles are such a ubiquitous and powerful part of erotic life. Of course, all of this sounds great, if not a bit broad and perhaps overambitious for the 1990s, if not also for today. But as Wolf's essay shifted toward sex itself, or what radical heterosexuality might look like "in bed," she doubled down on gender essentialism, imagining similarity and identification as antithetical to straightness, reserved only for lesbian and gay relationships. Wolf proclaimed, "I want the love of two unlikes. . . . These manifestations of difference confirm in heterosexuals the beauty that similarity confirms in the lesbian or gay imagination. Difference and animality do not have to mean hierarchy." Wolf went on to explain that women and men are so different, at least so differently socialized, that they are, for all intents and purposes, in a "cross-cultural relationship."[18]

This logic remains quite popular today, notably in the work of the internationally best-selling author Esther Perel, a relationship therapist known for recirculating the familiar argument that sexual desire is weakened by intimacy and identification. Perel explains, "Love enjoys knowing everything about you; desire needs mystery. Love likes to shrink the distance that exists between me and you, while desire is energized by it. If intimacy grows through repetition and familiarity, eroticism is numbed by repetition. It thrives on the mysterious, the novel, and the unexpected."[19] The notion that the erotic depends on distance and unfamiliarity, or "keeping the mystery alive," is one of the conceptual anchors of the heterosexual-repair industry, probably due to its resonance with the gender binary (for instance, a peddler of heterosexual repair might say, "It's a good thing that men and women are from two different planets. . . . It may lead to some miscommunication and resentment, but it keeps things hot!"). Of course, gender differences *are* sexy—in queer relationships, too—but in straight culture these differences are almost always taken to be essential, unchangeable, and of great consequence. They are imagined to be so significant as to produce inevitable cross-cultural misunderstandings and tense encounters, battles even, between people from two different planets. They are believed to cultivate the attraction of "opposites" and to inhibit identification and sameness.

Lesbian feminists and gay-liberation activists challenged this logic by arguing that their eroticism was actually forged *through* identification; when women had sex with women or men had sex with men, they discovered what was desirable about themselves through the mirror of their partners' bodies and desires. As in Audre Lorde's description of the erotic meeting of joyful equals, lesbian feminists argued that lesbian sex represented a kind of feminist praxis wherein lust and identification were not mutually exclusive but radically interconnected. Harry Hay, the early gay-liberation activist, called this praxis "subject-to-subject consciousness" and believed it was impossible within straight culture, wherein sexual partners were perceived as "other."[20] But I believe this convergence could occur in heterosexual sex, wherein straight men might have the capacity to feel such enthusiastic and irrepressible desire for women that their energies flow in the direction of women. Straight men could be so deeply heterosexual, so drawn to women, as to be "woman identified," to see themselves mirrored in the faces, bodies, and lives of women.

For many lesbian feminists, to feel genuine lust for women involved an enthusiastic interest in what gave women sexual pleasure. Adrienne Rich and Andrea Dworkin called this orientation "antiphallic sexuality," or the decentering of sex acts principally organized around men's pleasure and women's accommodation. One place where we can find a clear example of this antiphallic sexuality is, perhaps ironically, in the sexual encounter of the stone butch and the femme. The stone butch is often defined by what she did *not* want to do—she did not wish to be penetrated or even to be sexually touched in some cases—but the lesbian writer Joan Nestle has highlighted what the stone butch *did* wish to do, to experience erotic gratification from her capacity to bring pleasure to women.[21] The irony here is that critics of butch/femme genders perceived the stone butch, with her masculine appearance and gestures, as the epitome of women's potential for male identification, a troubling mimicry of "phallic" heteromasculinity. But, Nestle asks, what could be further from straight men's approach to sex than determinedly decentering one's own body and defining sex as that which brings pleasure to women? I am not suggesting here that straight men become stone, or untouched, but rather that the figure of the stone butch symbolizes the possibility of erotic generosity and woman identification anchored in masculinity and (often) in the generous use of the dildo/phallus (or in straight men's case, the bio-dildo, also known as a penis).

For lesbian feminists, liking women also meant liking the whole woman, or the less coercively modified woman. Accounts of this expansive lust for women can be found in lesbian feminist memoirs, in which body fat, cancer scars, power exchange, disability, aging, radical activism, self-love, years of sexual experience deemed "slutty" in the straight world, and various forms of embodied "ridiculousness" are all fodder for lesbian feminist arousal. I offer a few examples:

Audre Lorde, in *Zami*, reverently describes Ginger, her first lover, as "gorgeously fat, with an open knowledge about her body's movement that was delicate and precise. . . . She had pads of firm fat upon her thighs, and round dimpled knees. . . . Loving Ginger that night was like coming home to a joy I was meant for." Lorde later describes her lust for a different woman, Eudora, whose "pale keloids of radiation burn" were part of her irresistible body: "If I did not put my mouth upon hers and inhale the spicy smell of her breath my lungs would burst. . . . I looked from her round firm breast with its rosy nipple to her scarred chest. . . . I bent and kissed her softly upon the scar. . . . The pleasure of our night flushed over me like sun on the walls." By contrast, Lorde describes sex with men in terms similar to those used by many feminist straight women of her generation; sex with men was "pretty dismal and frightening and a little demeaning."[22]

Dorothy Allison, illuminating her gleeful dis/identification with the phallus, recounts her pleasure in "fucking, fucking, fucking" Alix, a woman who wore a dildo named "Bubba," a cock "fat and bent": "[It] jiggles obscenely when she walks around the room. Obscene and ridiculous, still no less effective when she puts it between my legs." Allison goes on to detail the shifting power dynamics between her and Alix, evoking her erotic identification with the vilified old woman, the crone: "She is ten years younger than me . . . sometimes. Sometimes I am eight and she is not born yet, but the ghost of her puts a hand on my throat, pinches my clit, bites my breast. . . . When I am fucking her, I am a thousand years old, a crone with teeth. . . . She is a suckling infant, soft in my hands, trusting me with her tender open places."[23]

Highlighting the lesbian feminist disinvestment in female sexual innocence and modesty, Jeanne Cordova recalls that her status as a handsome butch lesbian and high-profile radical organizer "brought dozens of women" to her bed, one of whom, Bejo, Cordova describes as "the most accomplished femme lover" she'd ever met. "Old-school bar femmes were far better lovers than newly coined lesbian feminists."[24]

Cherríe Moraga, too, desires a woman with age, accomplishment. Of Elena, the woman she lusts for, Moraga states, "I am ready for you now. I want age. Knowledge. Your body that still, after years, withholds and surrenders— keeps me there, waiting, wishing. . . . Willing. Willing to feel this time what disrupts in me. Girl. Woman. Child. Boy. Willing to embody what I will in the space of her arms."[25]

Lesbian feminist desire, in these accounts, is defined not purely by two women's sexual attraction to each other but by a *quality* of desiring women in which the objects of one's lust are women's complexities and accomplishments, both corporeal and otherwise. The best women lovers have the scars, the hunger, the weight, the teeth, and the political and sexual experience that allows them to know and harness their erotic will. Through Lorde's desiring gaze, physical features that are often cast as deeroticizing imperfections in the straight world are remade into sites of pleasure. In Allison's writing, sex with women is transformative and dead serious in its intensity, but it is also an inevitable send-up to the phallocentric self-seriousness of heteronormativity. In Cordova's retelling of her life story, there is no erotic without the movement, the revolution, and the battle scars and street cred earned by women at its helm. In Moraga's account, her lust is shot through with desire for the fruits of her lover's lived experience.

I dare say that this way of loving women, this understanding of the erotic, need not be owned by lesbians but is among the basic requirements of deep heterosexuality, wherein men's lust for women is triggered by women's actual temperaments, bodies, and experiences. Men's sense of being sexually orientated toward women must signal, as it does for most lesbians, an acute interest and investment in women's lives and accomplishments because, within deep heterosexuality, attraction is measly and half-baked if it is not a synthesis of lust and humanization. From this viewpoint, the hyperstraight man possesses an unstoppable interest not only in women's bodies but also in women's collective freedom. To be *into* women, one must be *for* women. To be an authentically straight man, or a deep heterosexual—and not a pseudoheterosexual who uses women to impress men—one must be a feminist.

## It Can Get Better

The discourse surrounding queer suffering and the ease of heterosexuality reflects a certain kind of reality, but it also obscures another. It masks the gendered suffering produced by straight culture, as well as queer sensations of freedom that result from having escaped not homophobia but heterosexual misery. My hope is that three main conclusions can be taken away from this project. The first point is that the normalization of violence and mutual dislike was central to straight culture from its modern inception, and even when this was recognized as a problem, efforts to address it simply reproduced the same binaristic, subject/object frameworks that undergirded the problem in the first place. The important point here is that while many people remain attached to the notion that embracing men's and women's purportedly unchangeable and complementary differences is the key to heterosexual harmony, this framework has never made a dent in the violence and misogyny that cause straight people to suffer. It is an unworkable foundation on which to build a sexual orientation. The suggestion I offer here, that straight men consider woman identification, or subject-subject eroticism, is one alternative.

Second, we cannot underestimate the capacity of neoliberal projects, like the self-help movement, to repackage and monetize feminist ideas, reducing them to matters of self-interest and economic exchange. As I have shown, the heterosexual-repair industry has turned to feminist concepts—about consent, male privilege, and toxic masculinity—to train men to be less offensive and seemingly more empathic, in the service of seducing women or managing their own public image. I anticipate that this trend will continue and expand. It can be seen, for instance, in recent headlines about powerful men seeking redemption and a return to their former financial success, following accusations of sexual harassment and public accountability in the context of #metoo.[26] Ultimately, this approach is anchored in straight men's self-interest, or what they can extract from women—often by exchanging empathy and decency for sex or forgiveness. From a queer feminist perspective, this is an example of the fragile and illusory character of straight life, wherein interest and identification must be faked. As an ally to straight people, I wish for them that their lust for one another might be genuinely born out of mutual regard and solidarity.

Lastly, queer people—and dykes in particular—are keen observers of the tragedy of heterosexuality. And we are *already* engaged in the work of alliance: as prochoice activists, sex educators, staff at women's centers, rape crisis advocates, and confidants for straight women in distress. We would not be doing this work if we didn't know that another way is possible. We know that straight men could be so attracted to women that they might as well rename their sexual orientation, recognizing that the term *feminist*, and not *straight*, is the best way to describe the expansiveness of their desires for women. We know that it is, in fact, the only way to truly capture how fully straight men could desire to love and lust for women, to live and struggle alongside women. We know, too, that straight women, for their part, must be bold enough to expect this from men, to demand so much more of straight men's ostensible love of women. Men who say they love women need to show women the receipts. They *can* do it. You *can* do it. We are here for you.

# Acknowledgments

THIS BOOK IS THE PRODUCT OF MANY EXHILARATING conversations, only some of which occurred in real life. The others took place in my imagination, in dialogue with bold and brilliant lesbian feminist writers who are no longer with us—may they rest in power. It also reflects many feminist chats with straight-identified friends, students, and colleagues. Thank you to everyone who answered thoughtfully when I asked questions like "Can you explain to me in detail why you are straight?"

The LA-based queer feminist writing group Lezerati is the birthplace of my ideas for this book and where it ultimately took form. My deep gratitude goes to Lynn Ballen, Robin Podolsky, Judith Branzburg, Talia Mae Bettcher, Alicia Vogl Saenz, Claudia Rodriguez, and Sam Cohen for their inspiration and straightforward feedback. I don't know how anyone writes a book without several razor-sharp and supportive dykes in their corner.

Thanks also to my friends and colleagues who talked through ideas, read drafts, or listened to me present this work and gave me their excellent feedback: Tey Meadow, Angela Jones, Jack Halberstam, Amin Ghaziani, Eric Stanley, C. J. Pascoe, Jade Sasser, Moon Charania, Brandon Robinson, Todd Reeser, Lisa Brush, Elsie Rivas-Gomez, Amy Tahani-Bidmeshki, and Shawn Schulenberg. Thank you to the organizers and participants at the American Men's Studies Association annual conference—Frank Karioris, Jonathan Allan, Andrea Waling, Kristen Barber, Jeffrey McCune, Tristan Bridges—who provided comments that shaped chapter 3. Special thanks are due to the editors of the NYU Press Sexual Cultures series, especially Ann Pellegrini, for their continued support of my writing, and to my editor, the ever-fabulous Ilene Kalish, for her many readings of this book and her embrace of my weird sense of humor.

Without a beloved community and family, I cannot write. Thank you to Layla Welborn, Vassilisa Kapila, Mel Dase, Rachel Luft, Gloria Williamson, Rachel Hall, Maren Ross, Steven Ross, Shirley Ward, Alex Ward, and Laurie Gow for the love and connection that provide the necessary balance to my work life.

And to Kat and Yarrow, my anchors: thank you for valuing queer and feminist ways of life as much as I do. I love you both so much.

# Notes

## Chapter 1. Let's Call It What It Is

1. Barbara Smith, "Toward a Black Feminist Criticism," *Women's Studies International Quarterly* 2, no. 2 (1979): 183–194.
2. Brittney Cooper, *Eloquent Rage: A Black Feminist Discovers Her Superpower* (New York: St. Martin's, 2018), 25.
3. Jasbir Puar, "In the Wake of It Gets Better," *The Guardian*, November 16, 2010, www.theguardian.com.
4. For the depressing evidence, see Darcy Lockman, *All the Rage: Mothers, Fathers, and the Myth of Equal Partnership* (New York: Harper, 2019).
5. I am using the terms "queer feminist" and "lesbian feminist" interchangeably here. While in some cases I do this to signal the revolutionary and counternormative sexual politics of many lesbian feminist activists writing in the 1970s and '80s (see Roderick Ferguson's book *One Dimensional Queer* [Medford, MA: Polity, 2018] for more on this), I also note that some lesbian feminists, including Cherríe Moraga and Gloria Anzaldúa, referred to themselves as "queer" in their early writing, years before the early 1990s emergence of queer as a widely embraced political umbrella. Gloria Anzaldúa, *Borderlands / La Frontera: The New Mestiza* (San Francisco: Aunt Lute Books, 1987); Cherríe Moraga, *Loving in the War Years* (Boston: South End, 1983). I am also using "queer/lesbian" as an umbrella term designed to signal a very broad range of queer feminist critiques that have called themselves "lesbian and . . . [fill in the blank]." Akin to the trans* use of the asterisk, we might imagine queer/lesbian as lesbian*: the term evokes many varying identifications and modes of critique that have understood themselves to fall within the category lesbian. Thank you to Lynn Ballen for drawing my attention to lesbian* uses of the asterisk.
6. The violence of heterosexual relationships was a core issue for lesbian feminists during the gay-liberation era, but it arguably became less central to later queer thinkers who turned their attention to the urgency of AIDS-phobic, antiqueer, anti-Black, and antitrans violence of state institutions and to the various ways that queer people survive and resist. The popularity of bioevolutionary theories of sexual orientation in the 1990s and early 2000s also chipped away at the notion that every woman was a potential lesbian (the "political lesbian" hypothesis); the majority of Americans now believe that we are born with an unchangeable heterosexual, homosexual, or bisexual constitution. Straight people's homophobic

contempt for LGBT people, fueled in the 1980s and '90s by the AIDS epidemic and conservative "family values" campaigns, also did not help inspire queer people's sympathies for straight women's gendered and sexual suffering. For all of these reasons, the lesbian feminist conversation about what feminist straight women should do with their desire for men, and vice versa, died on the vine by the 1990s, rendering straight people's problems seemingly irrelevant—if not also a bit satisfying—to queers.

7. The Radicalesbians, "The Woman-Identified Woman," in *Out of the Closets: Voices of Gay Liberation*, ed. Karla Jay and Allen Young (New York: NYU Press, 1972), 178.

8. "Mary" (anonymous), "A Letter from Mary," ibid., 178.

9. Audre Lorde, *Zami: A New Spelling of My Name* (Berkeley, CA: Crossing, 1982), 104.

10. Anzaldúa, *Borderlands / La Frontera*, 39, 41.

11. Kate Millet, *Sexual Politics* (New York: Columbia University Press, 1969).

12. Moraga, *Loving in the War Years*, 102.

13. Andrea Dworkin, *Our Blood: Prophecies and Discourses on Sexual Politics* (New York: Perigee Books, 1987), xi.

14. bell hooks, *Feminism Is for Everybody: Passionate Politics* (Boston: South End, 2000), 67.

15. Combahee River Collective, "Combahee River Collective Statement" (1977), in *Home Girls: A Black Feminist Anthology*, ed. *Barbara Smith* (New Brunswick, NJ: Rutgers University Press, 2000), 266.

16. See Anzaldúa, *Borderlands*; and Moraga, *Loving in the War Years*. In 2013, the Black queer women founders of the Black Lives Matter movement described this as a continuing problem: "Black liberation movements in this country have created room, space, and leadership mostly for Black heterosexual, cisgender men—leaving women, queer and transgender people, and others either out of the movement or in the background to move the work forward with little or no recognition." See Black Lives Matter, "Herstory," accessed December 11, 2019, https://blacklivesmatter.com.

17. Michelle Wallace, *Black Macho and the Myth of the Super Woman* (1978; repr., New York: Verso, 2015), 16 (emphasis in original).

18. Moraga, *Loving in the War Years*; Anzaldúa, *Borderlands*; Carla Trujillo, *Chicana Lesbians: The Girls Our Mothers Warned Us About* (Berkeley, CA: Third Woman, 1991).

19. Dorothy Allison, *Skin: Talking about Sex, Class, and Literature* (Ithaca, NY: Firebrand Books, 1994).

20. Gay Revolution Party Women's Caucus, "Realesbians and Politicalesbians," in Jay and Young, *Out of the Closets*, 178.

21. Jill Johnston, "The Comingest Womanifesto," in *Admission Accomplished: The Lesbian Nation Years (1970–75)* (Collingdale, PA: Diane, 1998), 212.

22. Adrienne Rich, "Compulsory Heterosexuality and Lesbian Existence," *Signs* 5, no. 4 (1980): 631–660.

23. For more on the patriarchal bargain, see Deniz Kandiyoti, "Bargaining with Patriarchy," *Gender & Society* 2, no. 3 (1988): 274–290; and Carole Pateman, *The Sexual Contract* (Stanford, CA: Stanford University Press, 1988).

24. Karen Martin, "Hetero-romantic Love and Heterosexiness in Children's G-Rated Films," *Gender & Society* 23, no. 3 (2009): 315–336.

25. Lorena Garcia, *Respect Yourself, Protect Yourself: Latina Girls and Sexual Identity* (New York: NYU Press, 2012).

26. See C. J. Pascoe's examination of high-school-aged boys' sex talk and its focus on what is abject about girls bodies in *Dude, You're a Fag* (Berkeley: University of California Press, 2007).

27. Michael Flood, "Men, Sex, and Homosociality: How Bonds between Men Shape Their Sexual Relations with Women," *Men and Masculinities* 10, no. 3 (2007): 339–359; Sharon Bird, "Welcome to the Men's Club: Homosociality and the Maintenance of Hegemonic Masculinity," *Gender & Society* 10, no. 2 (1996): 120–132.

28. Mireille Miller-Young, *A Taste for Brown Sugar: Black Women in Pornography*, (Durham, NC: Duke University Press, 2014).

29. Eve Kosofsky Sedgwick, *Between Men: English Literature and Male Homosocial Desire* (1985; repr., New York: Columbia University Press, 2015).

30. See Leta Hong Fincher, *Leftover Women: The Resurgence of Gender Inequality in China* (London: Zed Books, 2014). For the US context, see Susan Faludi's *Backlash: The Undeclared War on American Women* (1991; repr., New York: Broadway Books, 2006).

31. Lockman, *All the Rage.*

32. Gloria González-López, *Family Secrets: Stories of Incest and Sexual Violence in Mexico* (New York: NYU Press, 2015).

33. Diana Scully, "Convicted Rapists' Perceptions of Self and Victim: Role Taking and Emotions," *Gender & Society* 2, no. 2 (1988): 200–213.

34. Beth Richie, *Compelled to Crime: The Gender Entrapment of Battered Black Women* (New York: Routledge, 1995).

35. See Haunani-Kay Trask, *From a Native Daughter: Colonialism and Sovereignty in Hawai'i* (Honolulu: University of Hawaii Press, 1999); Audra Simpson, *Mohawk Interruptus: Political Life Across the Borders of Settler States* (Durham, NC: Duke University Press, 2014), chap. 6; and Hilary Weaver, "The Colonial Context of Violence: Reflections on Violence in the Lives of Native American Women," *Journal of Interpersonal Violence* 24, no. 9 (2008): 1552–1563.

36. See, for instance, JoAnn Wypijewski. "Primitive Heterosexuality: From Steubenville to the Marriage Altar," *The Nation*, April 9, 2013; Rebecca Traister, "Why Sex That's Consensual Can Still Be Bad," *The Cut*, October 20, 2015; Jessica Valenti, "Elliot Rodgers' Shooting Spree: Further Proof That Misogyny Kills," *The*

*Guardian*, May 24, 2014; Susan Rohwer, "It's Time to Silence 'GamerGate,' End the Misogyny in Gamer Culture," *Los Angeles Times*, October 17, 2014.

37. Shamita Das Dasgupta and Sujata Warrier, "In the Footsteps of Arundhati: Asian Indian Women's Experience of Domestic Violence in the United States," *Violence Against Women* 2, no. 3 (1996): 238–259.

38. See Sunny Woan, "White Sexual Imperialism: A Theory of Asian Feminist Jurisprudence," *Washington & Lee Journal of Civil Rights and Social Justice* 14, no. 2 (2007): 275–301; Kat Chow, "Odds Favor White Men, Asian Women on Dating Apps," National Public Radio, November 30, 2013, www.npr.org.

39. Traister, "Why Sex."

40. Kim Wallen and Elisabeth Lloyd, "Female Sexual Arousal: Genital Anatomy and Orgasm in Intercourse," *Hormones and Behavior* 59, no. 5 (2011): 780–792.

41. Martha McCaughey, *The Caveman Mystique* (New York: Routledge, 2008).

42. Melanie Heath, "Soft-Boiled Masculinity: Renegotiating Gender and Racial Ideologies in the Promise Keepers," *Gender & Society* 17, no. 3 (2003): 423–444.

43. Susan Faludi, *Backlash: The Undeclared War against American Women* (1991; repr., New York: Broadway Books, 2006); Arlie Hochschild, *The Second Shift: Working Families and the Revolution at Home* (1989; repr., New York: Penguin Books, 2003).

44. Jane Ward, *Not Gay: Sex between Straight White Men* (New York: NYU Press, 2015).

45. For a reprinting and analysis of correspondence from gay male readers for *Not Gay*, see Jane Ward, "Dyke Methods: A Meditation on Queer Studies and the Gay Men Who Hate It," *Women's Studies Quarterly* 44, nos. 3–4 (2016): 68–85.

46. Erin Sullivan, "Are Straight Women Okay?," *Autostraddle*, March 23, 2017, www.autostraddle.com.

47. Erin Sullivan, "It Appears Straight Women Are Not Okay," *Autostraddle*, June 8, 2017, www.autostraddle.com.

48. For research suggesting that the old adage that "it's funny because it's true" may be accurate, see Robert Lynch, "It's Funny Because We Think It's True: Laughter Is Augmented by Implicit Preferences," *Evolution and Human Behavior* 31, no. 2 (2010): 141–148.

49. Beth Eck, "Men Are Much Harder: Gendered Viewing of Nude Images," *Gender & Society* 17, no. 4 (2003): 691–710.

50. Reina Gattuso, "What I Would Have Said to You Last Night Had You Not Cum and Then Fallen Asleep," *Feministing*, August 4, 2016, http://feministing.com.

51. Lea Winerman, "Helping Men to Help Themselves," *APA Monitor on Psychology* 36, no. 7 (2005): 57.

52. Melanie Hamlett, "Men Have No Friends and Women Bear the Burden," *Harper's Bazaar*, May 2, 2019, www.harpersbazaar.com.

53. Ibid.

54. Cooper, *Eloquent Rage*, 23, 25.

55. Ward, *Not Gay*, 31.
56. Judith Butler, *Gender Trouble: Feminism and the Subversion of Identity* (London: Routledge, 1990).
57. Tristan Bridges and C. J. Pascoe, "Hybrid Masculinities: New Directions in the Sociology of Men and Masculinities," *Sociology Compass* 8, no. 3 (2014): 246–258.
58. Rich, "Compulsory Heterosexuality," 637.
59. Hanna Rosin, *The End of Men: And the Rise of Women* (New York: Riverhead Books, 2012).
60. Jack Halberstam, *Gaga Feminism: Sex, Gender, and the End of Normal* (New York: Beacon, 2013), 47.
61. Fincher, *Leftover Women*. A fascinating component of Fincher's analysis is the role of the Chinese state in inciting women's fear of being "leftover" (or never married). A popular *Xinhua News* column on the subject was reposted by several government media sites including the All-China Women's Federation website. The column warned, "[Women] excessively pursue perfection. The problem is that many of these women are too clear-headed, they can't tolerate weakness in their partner, especially since more and more women seek the 'three highs'—high education, high professional achievement and high income. Their standards for their careers and partners are so high, that by the time they want to marry, they discover that almost all of the men who are their equal in education and age are already married. For the group of white-collar women who don't find a partner, loneliness is a common occurrence. As these unmarried women age, the feeling of loneliness gets worse and worse."
62. D. A. Frederick, H. K. S. John, J. R. Garcia, and E. A. Lloyd, "Differences in Orgasm Frequency among Gay, Lesbian, Bisexual, and Heterosexual Men and Women in a U.S. National Sample," *Archives of Sexual Behavior* 47, no. 1(2018): 273.
63. Melanie Brewster, "Lesbian Women and Household Labor Division: A Systematic Review of Scholarly Research from 2000 to 2015," *Journal of Lesbian Studies* 21, no. 1 (2017): 47–69.
64. Marieka Klawitter, "Meta Analysis of the Effects of Sexual Orientation on Earnings," *Industrial Relations: Journal of Economy and Society* 54, no. 1 (2015): 4–32.
65. Nanette Gartrell, Amalia Deck, and Carla Rodas, "Adolescents with Lesbian Mothers Describe Their Own Lives," *Journal of Homosexuality* 59, no. 9 (2012): 1211–1229.
66. Francisco Perales and Janeen Baxter, "Sexual Identity and Relationship Quality in Australia and the United Kingdom," *Family Relations* 67, no. 1 (2017): 55–69.
67. Andrew Gelman, "Same Sex Divorce Rate Not as Low as It Seemed," *Washington Post*, December, 15, 2014, www.washingtonpost.com.
68. Taylor N. T. Brown and Jody L. Herman, *Intimate Partner Violence and Sexual Abuse Among LGBT People: A Review of Existing Research* (Los Angeles: Williams

Institute, 2015), https://williamsinstitute.law.ucla.edu; see also Sarah Schulman's book *Conflict Is Not Abuse: Overstating Harm, Community Responsibility, and the Duty of Repair* (New York: Arsenal Pulp, 2016) for a nuanced discussion of LGBT intimate-partner violence reporting.

69. See Tanya McNeil, "A Nation of Families: The Codification and (Be)Longings of Heteropatriarchy," in *Toward a Sociology of the Trace*, ed. Herman Gray and Macarena Gomez-Barris (Minneapolis: University of Minnesota Press, 2010), 57–86.

70. See Maggie Hadleigh-West's 1998 documentary *The War Zone* (Film Fatale Inc.) for footage of these interactions between men and women on public streets.

71. See C. J. Pascoe's ethnography of "River High," *Dude, You're a Fag*, in which she documents how boys' stories about sex were frequently detached from any positive erotic meanings, including their own personal pleasure or orgasm. Instead, mastery and conquest of girls' abject bodies took center stage in their tales. Boys' stories emphasized what they found disgusting about girls bodies (namely, blood, farts, and feces), and these stories included violent imagery of ripping vaginal walls and making girls bleed.

72. Jason Schultz, "Getting Off on Feminism," in *To Be Real: Telling the Truth and Changing the Face of Feminism*, ed. Rebecca Walker (New York: Anchor Books, 1995), 107–126.

73. *Dreamworlds 3: Desire, Sex, and Power in Music Video*, directed by Sut Jhally (Media Education Foundation, 2007).

74. Arlie Russell Hochschild, *Strangers in Their Own Land: Anger and Mourning on the American Right* (New York: New Press, 2016); see also Jason DeParle's review of Hochschild's book: "Book Review: Why Do People Who Need Help from the Government Hate It So Much?," *New York Times*, September 19, 2016, www.nytimes.com.

75. Lauren Berlant, *Cruel Optimism* (Durham, NC: Duke University Press, 2011), 2, 24.

## Chapter 2. He's Just Not That into You

1. See Silvia Federici, *Caliban and the Witch: Women, the Body and Primitive Accumulation* (New York: Autonomedia, 2004); Gayle Rubin, "The Traffic in Women: Notes on the Political Economy of Sex" (1975), in *The Second Wave: A Reader in Feminist Theory*, ed. Linda Nicholson (New York: Routledge, 1997), 27–62.

2. See Hanne Blank's book *Straight: The Surprisingly Short History of Heterosexuality* (New York: Beacon, 2012) for a pre-twentieth-century overview of the long and controversial emergence of heterosexual romantic love.

3. Men and women have coupled—in sex and in marriage—for centuries, but "being heterosexual" is a modern development. The terms "heterosexuality" and "homosexuality" were not invented until the late nineteenth century, when they appeared in European medical journals, and it would be decades later before they

embedded themselves in medical, legal, religious, and state institutions in Europe and the United States and subsequently became tools of imperial influence across the globe. See Jane Ward, *Not Gay: Sex between Straight White Men* (New York: NYU Press, 2015), for a review of this history.

4. Afsaneh Najmabadi, *Women with Mustaches and Men without Beards: Gender and Sexual Anxieties of Iranian Modernity* (Berkeley: University of California Press, 2005).

5. Ibid., 159.

6. Ibid., 156, 160.

7. See Charlotte Perkins Gilman, *Women and Economics* (Boston: Small, Maynard, 1898), for a first-wave feminist account of romantic marriage as false promise, a lure that seduces women into providing free labor. See also Blank, *Straight*; Rubin, "Traffic in Women"; Deniz Kandiyoti, "Bargaining with Patriarchy," *Gender & Society* 2, no. 3 (1988): 274–290; Jonathan Ned Katz, *The Invention of Heterosexuality* (Chicago: University of Chicago Press, 1995), for a historical overview of the modern campaign for heterosexuality; and Stephanie Coontz, *The Way We Never Were: American Families and the Nostalgia Trap* (New York: Basic Books, 1993), for a historical debunking of romanticized notions of marriage in the United States.

8. Rubin, "Traffic in Women," 38.

9. Marilyn Katz, "Ideology and the Status of Women in Ancient Greece," *History and Theory* 31, no. 4 (1992): 70–97; David Halperin, *One Hundred Years of Homosexuality: And Other Essays on Greek Love* (New York: Routledge, 1989). Also see the queer theorist Eve Sedgwick, who argues in *Between Men: English Literature and Male Homosocial Desire* (New York: Columbia University Press, 1985) that love and sexual intimacy among men and boys in ancient Greece did not threaten men's power but served patriarchal interests: "for the Greeks, that continuum between men loving men and men promoting the interests of men appears to have been quite seamless" (4).

10. Blank, *Straight*, 70–72.

11. Ward, *Not Gay*.

12. The number of marriage manuals produced in the early twentieth century was small enough that I was able to access all of the most impactful, or widely cited, texts. As this genre expanded into the mid- and late twentieth century, I have focused on best sellers, texts with international audiences, and other iconic examples from popular culture.

13. Julian Carter, *The Heart of Whiteness: Normal Sexuality and Race in America* (Durham, NC: Duke University Press, 2007).

14. Marriage laws and forced sterilization were strategies used to discourage childbearing within "unfit" communities.

15. Havelock Ellis, *Studies in the Psychology of Sex*, vol. 3, *Analysis of the Sexual Impulse* (1903), excerpted in *Sexology Uncensored: The Documents of Sexual*

*Science*, ed. Lucy Bland and Laura Doan (Chicago: University of Chicago Press, 1998), 108–109.

16. Lesley Hall, "Introduction to Part IV," ibid., 108.

17. Marie Stopes, *Married Love* (1918), excerpted ibid., 118.

18. Ibid., 119.

19. Ellis, *Studies*, 115.

20. William Robinson, *Married Life and Happiness; or, Love and Comfort in Marriage* (New York: Eugenics Publishing, 1922), 25–26.

21. Howard W. Long, *Sane Sex Life and Sane Sex Living* (New York: Eugenics Publishing, 1919), 60.

22. John Stokes, *The Third Great Plague: A Discussion of Syphilis for Everyday People* (Philadelphia: W. B. Saunders, 1920), 26; Elie Metchnikoff, *The New Hygiene: Three Lectures on the Prevention of Infectious Disease* (Chicago: W. T. Keener, 1907), 77; Christina Simmons, "African Americans and Sexual Victorianism in the Social Hygiene Movement, 1910–40," *Journal of the History of Sexuality* 4, no. 1 (1993): 71.

23. See Lilian Faderman, *Odd Girls and Twilight Lovers: A History of Lesbian Life in Twentieth-Century America* (New York: Penguin, 1991); George Chauncey, *Gay New York: Gender, Urban Culture, and the Making of the Gay Male World, 1890–1940* (New York: Basic Books, 1995).

24. Robinson, *Married Life*, 25–26.

25. Bernarr Macfadden, *Womanhood and Marriage* (New York: Physical Culture Corporation, 1918).

26. See Anne McClintock's discussion of the patriarchal and white-supremacist imagery in late nineteenth-century soap advertising, in *Imperial Leather: Race, Gender, and Sexuality in the Colonial Contest* (New York: Routledge, 1995).

27. Long, *Sane Sex Life*, 17.

28. Ibid., 19.

29. See Patricia Hill Collins, *Black Sexual Politics: African Americans, Gender, and the New Racism* (New York: Routledge, 2005); and Julian Carter, *The Heart of Whiteness: Normal Sexuality and Race in America* (Durham, NC: Duke University Press, 2007).

30. Katherine Franke, *Wedlocked: The Perils of Marriage Equality* (New York: NYU Press, 2015).

31. Simmons, "African Americans and Sexual Victorianism," 71.

32. For a thorough and fascinating account of this partnership between male physicians and early feminists, see Christina Simmons, *Making Marriage Modern: Women's Sexuality from the Progressive Era to World War II* (Oxford: Oxford University Press, 2009).

33. See Barbara Welter, "The Cult of True Womanhood: 1820–1860," *American Quarterly* 18, no. 2 (1966): 151–174.

34. Hortense Spillers, *Black, White, and in Color* (Chicago: University of Chicago Press, 2003), 203–229.

35. See Saidiya Hartman's stunning speculative history of the sexual modernism of freedom-seeking Black women in early twentieth-century American cities: *Wayward Lives, Beautiful Experiments* (New York: Norton, 2019). Hartman offers a counternarrative that resists white-supremacist characterizations of Black women at the turn of the century as "promiscuous, reckless, wild, and wayward," pointing instead to their utopian longings and feminist/queer innovations (xiii).

36. Some midcentury physician's manuals did continue to emphasize the possibility of new wives' repulsion at the idea of sex with their husbands. For instance, in Herman Pomeranz and Irvin Koll's *The Family Physician* (New York: Greystone, 1957), the authors assert that girls who have not been counseled about heterosexual sex "may be greatly shocked and even disgusted by sexual relations in marriage" (201).

37. Alfred Henry Tyrer, *Sex Satisfaction and Happy Marriage: A Practical Handbook* (New York: Emerson Books, 1951), 127, 129.

38. See Bettye Collier-Thomas and V. P. Franklin, eds., *Sisters in the Struggle: African-American Women in the Civil Rights-Black Power Movement* (New York: NYU Press, 2001); Bernice McNair Barnett, "Invisible Southern Black Women Leaders in the Civil Rights Movement," *Gender & Society* 7, no. 2 (1993): 162–182; Dennis Urban, "The Women of SNCC: Struggle, Sexism, and the Emergence of Feminist Consciousness, 1960–66," *International Social Science Review* 77, nos. 3–4 (2002): 185–190.

39. See Dorothy Height's essay "'We Wanted the Voice of a Woman to Be Heard': Black Women and the 1963 March on Washington," in Collier-Thomas and Franklin, *Sisters in the Struggle*, 83–92.

40. Money, quoted in Terry Goldie, *The Man Who Invented Gender: Engaging the Ideas of John Money* (Vancouver: University of British Columbia Press, 2014), 45.

41. "The happy housewife" was a popular midcentury American archetype, even as this fantasy was out of reach for many white women (who weren't made happy by heterosexual marriage) and an impossibility for many women of color, many of whom were employed in the service of white women's striving for heterosexual happiness (by working as maids, child-care providers, etc.). As the feminist theorist Sara Ahmed inquires in *The Promise of Happiness* (Durham, NC: Duke University Press, 2010), "How better to justify an unequal division of labor than to say that such labor makes people happy? How better to secure consent to unpaid or poorly paid labor than to describe such consent as the origin of good feeling?" (50).

42. Edward Podolsky, *Sex Today in Wedded Life: A Doctor's Confidential Advice* (New York: Simon, 1947), 236.

43. Michelle Wallace, *Black Macho and the Myth of the Superwoman*, (New York: Verso, 1990), 14.

44. Ibid., 15.

45. Daniel Greary, *Beyond Civil Rights: The Moynihan Report and Its Legacy* (Philadelphia: University of Pennsylvania Press, 2015).

46. Andrea Tone, *Devices and Desires: A History of Contraceptives in America* (New York: Macmillan, 2002).

47. "Young Man's Fancy," film advertisement produced by General Electric, 1952.

48. See, for instance, *Ebony*, November 1959, 121, 142.

49. Advertising in women's magazines also spoke directly to women's fears about their husbands' violence against children. For instance, to market a pediatric laxative, Fletcher's Castoria ads of 1939 and 1940 depicted wives protecting children from brutal fathers willing to use force to make children take their medicine. The ads, appearing in women's magazines such as *Redbook* and *Women's Home Companion*, linked gentle parenting—the responsibility of women—with the use of a gentle children's laxative.

50. See Bill Osgerby, *Playboys in Paradise: Masculinity, Youth, and Leisure Style in Modern America* (New York: Bloomsbury, 2001).

51. Varda Burstyn, *The Rites of Men: Manhood, Politics, and the Culture of Sport* (Toronto: University of Toronto Press, 1999), 130.

52. Paul B. Preciado, *Pornotopia: An Essay on Playboy's Architecture and Biopolitics* (Cambridge, MA: MIT Press, 2014).

53. *Marriage Today*, short film produced by McGraw-Hill, 1948. https://www.youtube.com/watch?v=BKfbDrYpcqw.

54. Joanne Meyerowitz, "Women, Cheesecake, and Borderline Material: Responses to Girlie Pictures in Mid-Twentieth-Century U.S.," *Journal of Women's History* 8, no. 3 (1996): 9–35.

55. By contrast, see Alexandra Chasin's *Selling Out: The Gay and Lesbian Movement Goes to Market* (New York: Palgrave Macmillan, 2001) for an investigation of the difficulties marketers encountered attempting to figure out how to commodify *lesbian* culture or to determine what might motivate lesbians to buy their products.

56. Jennifer Maher, "What Do Women Watch? Tuning In to the Compulsory Heterosexuality Channel," in *Reality TV: Remaking Television Culture*, ed. Susan Murray and Laurie Ouellette (New York: NYU Press, 2004), 197–213.

57. Robin Norwood, *Women Who Love Too Much: When You Keep Wishing and Hoping He'll Change* (1985; repr., New York: Pocket Books, 2008), xvii.

58. Ibid., 150.

59. Iyanla Vanzant, *In the Meantime: Finding Yourself and the Love You Want* (New York: Atria Books, 1998).

60. Susan Forward, *Men Who Hate Women and the Women Who Love Them: When Loving Hurts and You Don't Know Why* (New York: Bantam Books, 1986), 38.

61. Ibid., 98.

62. Ibid., 97.

63. Patricia Hill Collins, *Black Sexual Politics: African Americans, Gender, and the New Racism* (New York: Routledge, 2004), 51.

64. Kylie Murphy, "What Does John Gray Have to Say to Feminism?," *Continuum: Journal of Media and Cultural Studies* 15, no. 2 (2001): 159–167.

65. See Deniz Kandiyoti, "Bargaining with Patriarchy," *Gender & Society* 2, no. 3 (1988): 274–290.

66. Ibid., 280.

67. Gary Chapman, *The Five Love Languages: The Secret to Love That Lasts* (Chicago: Northfield, 1992), 38.

68. Sharon Hays, *The Cultural Contradictions of Motherhood* (New Haven, CT: Yale University Press, 1998).

69. Susan Maushart, *Wifework: What Marriage Really Means for Women* (New York: Bloomsbury, 2002). Quotes from the publisher's description of the book on its website: www.bloomsbury.com.

70. Brittney Cooper, *Eloquent Rage: A Black Feminist Discovers Her Superpower* (New York: St. Martin's, 2018), 234.

71. Steve Harvey, *Act Like Lady, Think Like a Man* (New York: Amistad, 2009), 42.

72. Eliza Anyangwe, "Misogynoir: Where Racism and Sexism Meet," *The Guardian*, October 5, 2015, www.theguardian.com.

73. Sherry Argov, *Why Men Love Bitches: From Doormat to Dreamgirl—A Woman's Guide to Holding Her Own in a Relationship* (New York: Adams Media, 2002), 77.

74. Hall, "Introduction to Part IV," 107.

75. See Bianca Williams, *The Pursuit of Happiness: Black Women, Diasporic Dreams, and the Politics of Emotional Transnationalism* (Durham, NC: Duke University Press, 2018); Elizabeth Bernstein, *Temporarily Yours: Intimacy, Authenticity, and the Commerce of Sex* (Chicago: University of Chicago Press, 2007); and Elif Batuman, "Japan's Rent-a-Family Industry," *New Yorker*, April 30, 2018, www.newyorker.com.

76. See the website Men Going Their Own Way, www.mgtow.com.

77. For a fascinating study of a megaevent designed to repair heterosexual men, see Melanie Heath, "Soft-Boiled Masculinity: Renegotiating Gender and Racial Ideologies in the Promise Keepers," *Gender & Society* 17, no. 3 (2003): 423–444.

78. According to Robbins's website, "Robbins has empowered more than 50 million people from 100 countries through his audio, video and life training programs. He created the #1 personal and professional development program of all time, and more than 4 million people have attended his live seminars." (Robbins's other credentials include being a personal adviser to President Bill Clinton and being named "CEO Whisperer" by *Fortune* magazine.) See "About Tony Robbins," Tony Robbins's website, www.tonyrobbins.com.

79. Some of these ideas have their origins in the mythopoetic men's movement of the 1980s. See Michael Messner, "'Changing Men' and Feminist Politics in the United States," *Theory and Society* 2, no. 5 (1993): 723–737.

## Chapter 3. Pickup Artists

1. But then again, perhaps the reference to the Bible is not entirely code. The *New York Times* best-selling book that launched the pickup-artist industry, Neil Strauss's *The Game* (New York: HarperCollins, 2005), has a black faux-leather cover, faux-gold-gilded pages, and a red-satin ribbon to mark one's favorite "passage." Passed among men as the essential handbook for successfully "sarging on HBs" (picking up hot babes), *The Game* has taken on the quality of a rare and sacred text—even as it is a click away on Amazon.com.

2. The owners of both companies enthusiastically agreed to allow me to observe their bootcamps free of charge, explaining that they would like to see the public have a more nuanced and accurate understanding of their work.

3. As Jack Halberstam has argued, popular film and television loves to pair unappealing men and remarkable women, with numerous Hollywood films often centered on ostensibly romantic situations in which "the stupider and more pathetic the male heroes become, the more they are loved by exceptional women." Halberstam, "Dumb Getting Dumber: Sideways, Spongebob, and the New Masculinity," *Bitch*, February 28, 2005, www.bitchmedia.org.

4. *Dreamworlds 3*, directed by Sut Jhally (Media Education Foundation, 2008), www.sutjhally.com.

5. Laura Kipnis, "Kick against the Pricks," *New York Review of Books*, December 21, 2017, www.nybooks.com.

6. Sarah Ratchford, a reporter for Vice, provided sympathetic coverage of pickup artists in her article "I Spoke to a Pick-Up Artist to See If They're as Bad as I Think They Are," *Vice*, July 9, 2014, www.vice.com; see also Rachel O'Neill, *Seduction: Men, Masculinity, and Mediated Intimacy* (Cambridge, UK: Polity, 2018).

7. During this exercise was the only instance in which a coach referred to my presence. Kezia, the lead coach, gestured at me and said, "See this woman over here, sitting quietly? I saw many of you speaking with her during the break. She has a PhD. Why are you not intimidated to speak with her but intimidated by a nineteen-year-old bimbo?" Though one of the men responded, "Well, we didn't know that about her," I knew from their previous comments that I, then in my late thirties, was well over their desired age.

8. Regarding socioeconomic status, seduction coaches commonly emphasize to their students that anyone can afford to take their classes if they are willing to make necessary sacrifices. They share stories about men who have gone into debt or scrimped and saved—one man reportedly slept in his car in order to save money on rent—in order to fund their seduction course work.

9. O'Neill, *Seduction*.

10. See Madeleine Davis, "An Easy Guide to Fending Off Pickup Artists," *Jezebel*, June 21, 2013, https://jezebel.com, for an especially funny critique of negs.

11. The incel community grew out of the pickup-artist movement, though incels often reject pickup artists for being "too humanizing" of women. "What Is An Incel?," *New York Times*, April 24, 2018, www.nytimes.com.

12. Malcolm Forbes and Ryan Anderson, "The Psychology of the Pickup Artist," *The Mating Game* (blog), *Psychology Today*, November 11, 2014, www.psychologyto-day.com.

13. Rafael Behr, "Girls, If You See This Man, Run a Mile," *The Guardian*, September 24, 2005, www.theguardian.com. For feminist analyses of the way that straight men are often motivated by homosocial and homoerotic bonding more so than heterosexual sex itself, see Peggy Reeves Sanday, *Fraternity Gang Rape: Sex, Brotherhood, and Privilege on Campus* (New York: NYU Press, 2007); and Jane Ward, *Not Gay: Sex between Straight White Men* (New York: NYU Press, 2015).

14. Sarah Ratchford, "I Tried to Find Out If Pickup Artists Are Still Influential in 2017," *Vice*, August 25, 2017, www.vice.com.

15. Elizabeth Haag, "The Secret World of Men," *Jezebel*, March 22, 2010, https://jezebel.com; Katie Baker, "Is There Such a Thing as a Feminist Pickup Artist?" *Jezebel*, June 25, 2013, https://jezebel.com.

16. Baker, "Is There Such a Thing as a Feminist Pickup Artist?"

17. Ratchford, "I Tried to Find Out."

18. Haag, "Secret World of Men."

19. O'Neill, *Seduction*, 17.

20. Jane Ward, "Gender Labor: Transmen, Femmes, and the Collective Work of Transgression," *Sexualities* 13, no. 2 (2010): 236–254.

21. Diana Scully, "Convicted Rapists' Perceptions of Self and Victim: Role Taking and Emotions," *Gender & Society* 2, no. 2 (1988): 200–213.

22. See Lisa Diamond's similar argument in *Sexual Fluidity: Understanding Women's Love and Desire*, (Cambridge, MA: Harvard University Press, 2009).

23. O'Neill, *Seduction*, 98.

24. Nicola Gavey, *Just Sex? The Cultural Scaffolding of Rape* (London: Routledge, 2005).

25. Ratchford, "I Tried to Find Out."

26. Melissa Davey, "U.S. Pickup Artist Julien Blanc Forced to Leave Australia after Visa Cancelled," *The Guardian*, November 7, 2014, www.theguardian.com; Alan Travis, "Julien Blanc Barred from Entering UK," *The Guardian*, November 19, 2014, www.theguardian.com.

27. Megan Gibson, "Is This the Most Hated Man in the World?," *Time*, November 4, 2014, http://time.com.

28. Ratchford, "I Tried to Find Out."

29. Ibid.

30. See Abby Ferber, "Racial Warriors and Weekend Warriors: The Construction of Masculinity in Mythopoetic and White Supremacist Discourse," *Men and Masculinities* 3, no. 1 (2000): 30–35.

31. Rebecca Traister, "Why Sex That's Consensual Sex Can Still Be Bad. And Why We're Not Talking about It," *Cut*, October 20, 2015, www.thecut.com.

32. Men Can Stop Rape has since eliminated this campaign due to such critiques. See its announcement, "Say Goodbye to 'My Strength Is Not for Hurting,'" *Men Can Stop Rape Blog*, December 14, 2011, http://mencanstoprape.blogspot.com; see also Tristan Bridges and C. J. Pascoe's analysis of this campaign as an example of "discursive distancing" in their 2014 article "Hybrid Masculinities: New Directions in the Sociology of Men and Masculinity," *Sociology Compass* 8, no. 3 (2014): 246–258.

33. O'Connell Davidson and Julia Sanchez-Taylor, "Travel and Taboo: Heterosexual Sex Tourism to the Caribbean," in *Regulating Sex: The Politics of Intimacy and Identity*, ed. Elizabeth Bernstein and Laurie Schaffner (London: Routledge, 2005), 83–100; Kimberly Kay Hoang, *Dealing in Desire: Asian Ascendancy, Western Declines, and the Hidden Currencies of Global Sex Work* (Berkeley: University of California Press, 2015); M. Jacqui Alexander, *Pedagogies of Crossing: Meditations on Feminism, Sexual Politics, Memory, and the Sacred* (Durham, NC: Duke University Press, 2006); Anne McClintock, *Imperial Leather: Race, Gender and Sexuality in the Colonial Contest* (New York: Routledge, 1995).

34. Eve Sedgwick, *Between Men: English Literature and Male Homosocial Desire* (New York: Columbia University Press, 1985), 21–27.

35. See Ward, *Not Gay*.

36. See Brandon Robinson, "'Personal Preference' as the New Racism: Gay Desire and Racial Cleansing in Cyberspace," *Sociology of Race & Ethnicity* 1, no. 2 (2015): 317–330.

37. Helen Smith, *Men on Strike: Why Men Are Boycotting Marriage, Fatherhood, and the American Dream* (New York: Encounter Books, 2014); Susan Faludi, *Backlash: The Undeclared War against Women* (New York: Broadway Books, 1991). See also the self-help books discussed in detail in chapter 2.

### Chapter 4. A Sick and Boring Life

*Epigraphs:* Jill Johnston, "Lois Lane Is a Lesbian" (1971), in *Admission Accomplished: The Lesbian Nation Years (1970–75)* (London: Serpent's Tale, 1998); Gloria Anzaldua, interview by AnnLouise Keating, October 25–26, 1991, published in *Frontiers*, September 22, 1993.

1. Beverly Daniel Tatum, *Why Are All the Black Kids Sitting Together in the Cafeteria? And Other Conversations about Race* (New York: Basic Books, 1997).

2. JoAnn Wypijewski, "Primitive Heterosexuality: From Steubenville to the Marriage Altar," *Nation*, April 9, 2013, www.thenation.com.

3. Paul Preciado, "Letter from a Tranman to the Old Sexual Regime," *Texte Zur Kunst*, January 22, 2018, www.textezurkunst.de.

4. James Baldwin, in the *Village Voice*, 1984, quoted in Jonathan Ned Katz, *The Invention of Heterosexuality* (Chicago: University of Chicago Press, 2007), 103.

5. The Radicalesbians, "The Woman-Identified Woman," in Out of the Closets: Voices of Gay Liberation, ed. Karla Jay and Allen Young (New York: NYU Press, 1972), 172.

6. Judith Butler, *Gender Trouble: Feminism and the Subversion of Identity* (London: Routledge, 1990), 70.

7. George Chauncey, *Gay New York: Gender, Urban Culture, and the Making of the Gay Male World, 1890–1940* (New York: Basic Books, 1995).

8. Marty Myron, *Daily Life in the United States, 1960–1990: Decades of Discord* (Westport, CT: Greenwood, 1997), 125, quoting *Time*, July 7, 1967, 20.

9. Wypijewski, "Primitive Heterosexuality."

10. Michelson offers a caveat that commonly accompanies these kinds of assertions and with which I agree: "I'm talking about straight people and culture—the collective, the institutional—not necessarily individual straight persons, many of whom are allies and friends and who would like to see a queer revolution as much as I would." Noah Michelson, "Why I Never Want to Be Just Like Straight People," *HuffPost*, December 11, 2013, www.huffpost.com.

11. I discarded one-word responses (namely, "yes" and "no") because I had no way of assessing their meaning.

12. Jane Ward, "Dyke Methods: A Meditation on Queer Studies and the Gay Men Who Hate It," *Women's Studies Quarterly* 44, nos. 3–4 (2016): 68–83; Ward, "The Methods Gatekeepers and the Exiled Queers," in *Other, Please Specify: Queer Methods in Sociology*, ed. D'Lane R. Compton, Tey Meadow, and Kristen Schilt (Berkeley: University of California Press, 2018), 51–66.

13. I asked respondents how they identify their race and gender, and I include these self-identifications alongside their responses.

14. Valerie Solanas, *SCUM Manifesto* (1967; repr., London: Verso, 2016), 35.

15. Butler, *Gender Trouble*.

16. Lee Edelman, *No Future: Queer Theory and the Death Drive* (Durham, NC: Duke University Press, 2004).

17. See John D'Emilio, "Capitalism and Gay Identity," in *The Lesbian and Gay Studies Reader*, ed. Henry Abelove, Michele Aina Barale, and David Halperin (New York: Routledge, 1993), 467–476; Michel Foucault, *The History of Sexuality, Part I* (Paris: Editions Gallimard, 1976); E Patrick Johnson, *Sweet Tea: Black Gay Men of the South* (Chapel Hill: University of North Carolina Press, 2011); Roderick Ferguson, *Aberrations in Black: Toward a Queer of Color Critique* (Minneapolis: University of Minnesota Press, 2003); Qwo-Li Driskill, Chris Finley, Brian Joseph Gilley, and Scott Lauria Morgensen, eds., *Queer Indigenous Studies: Critical Interventions in Theory, Politics, and Literature* (Tucson: University of Arizona Press, 2011).

18. Dayna Troisi and Corinne Werder, "70 Things Straight People Love," *GO*, October 2018, http://gomag.com.

19. Fourteen percent of LGBT voters are estimated to have voted for Donald Trump in 2016, compared with 53 percent of men and 42 percent of women in the general

population. See NBC News, "NBC News Exit Poll: Trump Fails to Peal LGBT Voters Away from Democratic Party," November 8, 2016, www.nbcnews.com; and BBC News, "Reality Check: Who Voted for Donald Trump?," November 9, 2016, www.bbc.com/news.

20. Troisi and Werder, "70 Things Straight People Love."
21. "Author: Dayna Troisi," *GO*, accessed December 11, 2019, http://gomag.com; "Author: Corinne Werder," *GO*, accessed December 11, 2019, hattp://gomag.com.
22. See Karen Tongson, "#Normporn," *Public Books*, August 1, 2015, www.public-books.org.
23. Lauren Berlant, *The Female Complaint: The Unfinished Business of Sentimentality in American Culture* (Durham, NC: Duke University Press, 2018).
24. Ibid., 5–6.
25. Melissa Harris-Perry, *Sister Citizen: Shame, Stereotypes, and Black Women in America* (New Haven, CT: Yale University Press, 2013).
26. See Jonathan Cobb and Richard Sennett, *The Hidden Injuries of Class* (New York: Norton, 1972).
27. Robin Podolsky, "Sacrificing Queers and Other Proletarian Artifacts," *Radical America* 25, no. 1 (1991): 57.
28. Sara Ahmed, *Living a Feminist Life* (Durham, NC: Duke University Press, 2017), 119.
29. Sara Ahmed, *The Promise of Happiness* (Durham, NC: Duke University Press, 2010), 88. Relatedly, Ahmed accounts here the story of Vin Packer, author of the first bestselling lesbian pulp novel *Spring Fire*, first published in 1952: "The novel will be published, but only on condition that it does not have a happy ending, as such an ending would 'make homosexuality attractive.'"
30. Adrienne Rich, "Compulsory Heterosexuality and Lesbian Existence," *Signs: Journal of Women in Culture and Society* 5, no. 4 (1986): 658.
31. Blythe Roberson, *How to Date Men When You Hate Men* (New York: Flatiron Books, 2018), 6.
32. Ibid., 7.
33. Ibid., 267.
34. See Barr's quote in Joe Kort, *Gay Affirmative Therapy for the Straight Clinician* (New York: Norton, 2008), 110.
35. Gemma Hartley, *Fed Up: Emotional Labor, Women, and the Way Forward* (New York: HarperCollins, 2018).
36. Samantha Rodman, "The Wife Who Wants More and Her Annoyingly Satisfied Husband," *Dr. Psych Mom* (blog), December 28, 2014, www.drpsychmom.com.
37. Kasey Edwards, "Why Having a Husband Can Be Like Having a Third Child," *Sydney Morning Herald*, March 11, 2018, www.smh.com.au.
38. Hannah Giorgis, "Do Beyoncé Fans Have to Forgive Jay-Z?," *Atlantic*, June 18, 2018, www.theatlantic.com.
39. Esther Newton and Shirley Waltons, "The Misunderstanding: Toward a More Precise Sexual Vocabulary" (1984), in *Margaret Mead Made Me Gay: Personal*

*Essays, Public Ideas,* by Esther Newton (Durham, NC: Duke University Press, 2000), 167.

40. Kate Bornstein, *Gender Outlaw: On Men, Women, and the Rest of Us* (New York: Vintage Books, 1994), 32.
41. Travers Scott, "Flexible Fidelity," in *Gay Men at the Millennium: Sex, Spirit, Community,* ed. Michael Lowenthal (New York: Tarcher/Putnam 1997), 72–73.
42. Monique Wittig, *The Straight Mind and Other Essays* (Boston: Beacon, 1992), 28.
43. José Esteban Muñoz, *Cruising Utopia: The Then and There of Queer Futurity* (New York: NYU Press, 2009).
44. Rich, "Compulsory Heterosexuality," 648.
45. Wittig, *Straight Mind,* 25.
46. "How Gay Should a Gay Bar Be?," *New York Times,* June 24, 2017, www.nytimes.com; Brock Thompson, "Women in Gay Bars: A Defense," *Washington Blade,* August 31, 2016, www.washingtonblade.com; Miz Cracker, "Beware the Bachelorette! A Report from the Straight Lady Invasion of Gay Bars," *Slate,* August 13, 2015, https://slate.com.
47. Miz Cracker, "Beware the Bachelorette!"
48. Angela Jones, "#DemandBetter Straight Sex!," *Bully Bloggers,* January 21, 2018, https://bullybloggers.wordpress.com.
49. Nicola Gavey, *Just Sex? The Cultural Scaffolding of Sex* (New York: Routledge, 2005).
50. Debby Herbenick, Tsung-Chieh (Jane) Fu, Jennifer Arter, Stephanie A. Sanders, and Brian Dodge, "Women's Experiences with Genital Touching, Sexual Pleasure, and Orgasm: Results from a U.S. Probability Sample of Women Ages 18 to 94," *Journal of Sex & Marital Therapy* 44, no. 2 (2018): 201–212.
51. David A. Frederick, H. Kate St. John, Justin R. Garcia, and Elisabeth A. Lloyd, "Differences in Orgasm Frequency among Gay, Lesbian, Bisexual, and Heterosexual Men and Women in a U.S. National Sample," *Archives of Sexual Behavior* 47, no. 1 (2018): 273–288.
52. See Joan Nestle's discussion of how butch masculinity, unlike heteromasculinity, is often oriented toward the sexual pleasure of femmes, in *The Persistent Desire: A Femme-Butch Reader* (New York: Alyson, 1992).
53. For a deep dive into this dynamic as it relates to vaginas after the age of fifty, see Darcey Steinke's *Flash Count Diary: Menopause and the Vindication of Natural Life* (New York: Sarah Crichton Books, 2019). Steinke offers the example of how a male doctor at a medical conference on menopause speaks about the vagina: "He talks of shrinkage, lack of pliability, dryness. All his descriptions explain how the vagina might feel to an incoming penis. The vagina as a viable penis holder. Not how a vagina might feel to the woman it belongs to" (163).

## Chapter 5. Deep Heterosexuality

1. See Ariane Cruz, *The Color of Kink: Black Women, BDSM, and Pornography* (New York: NYU Press, 2016).

2. For a review of much of this literature, see Angela Willey's introductory chapter in *Undoing Monogamy: The Politics of Science and the Possibilities of Biology* (Durham, NC: Duke University Press, 2016); see also Mimi Schippers, *Beyond Monogamy: Polyamory and the Future of Polyqueer Sexualities* (New York: NYU Press, 2016).

3. For instance, Charlie Glickman and Aislinn Emirzian argue in *The Ultimate Guide to Prostate Pleasure* (Minneapolis: Cleis, 2013) that pegging can build men's empathy for women, liberate men from elements of toxic masculinity, and fundamentally transform heterosexuality.

4. Jack Halberstam, *Gaga Feminism: Sex, Gender, and the End of Normal* (Boston: Beacon, 2012).

5. Jane Ward, *Not Gay: Sex between Straight White Men* (New York: NYU Press, 2015).

6. Audre Lorde, "The Uses of the Erotic: The Erotic as Power," in *Sister/Outsider: Essays and Speeches by Audre Lorde* (Berkeley, CA: Ten Speed, 1984), 54.

7. Eve Sedgwick, *Between Men: English Literature and Male Homosocial Desire* (New York: Columbia University Press, 1985); C. J. Pascoe, *Dude, You're a Fag: Masculinity and Sexuality in High School* (Berkeley: University of California Press, 2011); Ward, *Not Gay*.

8. In the 2009 "Deep Lez: Statement," Mitchell explains, "Deep Lez was coined to acknowledge the urgent need to develop inclusive libratory feminisms while examining the strategic benefits of maintaining some components of a radical lesbian theory and practice. . . . In so doing, 'lesbian' is resurrected as a potential site of radical identification, rather than one of de-politicized apathy (or worse, shame). . . . For example, the language of Deep Lez has been adopted by those at the Michigan Womyn's Music Festival who lobby for trans inclusion, as well as the organizers of Camp Trans, who use an article about Deep Lez in their annual trans solidarity packages. Here, Deep Lez is mobilized to move radical lesbianism and identification with or allegiance to trans communities out of the realm of either/or and into the space of both/and." Allyson Mitchell, "Deep Lez: Statement," *NoMorePotlucks*, 2009, http://nomorepotlucks.com. The feminist scholar Sara Ahmed, in her book *Living a Feminist Life* (Durham, NC: Duke University Press, 2016), also calls for a "revival of lesbian feminism," a returning to its archives to bring feminism "back to life" by centering the intersectional interventions of lesbian feminists of color and trans lesbian feminists (213–214).

9. I recognize that there is an irony in turning to elements of 1970s and '80s lesbian feminism as a model for heterosexuality. It is ironic because many lesbian feminists during this era agreed that heterosexuality—which required identification with men—was incompatible with feminist practice, and hence, they urged straight women to become "political lesbians" by leaving the men in their lives. Lesbianism, for many white, lesbian, feminist activists in particular, was feminism taken to its logical conclusion, or as Ti-Grace Atkinson reportedly proclaimed, feminism was the theory, lesbianism was the practice. In a similar vein, the group

Radicalesbians declared that feminism and lesbianism were inseparable in their 1970 manifesta "Woman-Identified Woman" (in *Out of the Closets: Voices of Gay Liberation*, ed. Karla Jay and Allen Young [New York: NYU Press, 1972]. A lesbian, the group boldly explained, was "the rage of all women condensed to the point of explosion" (172). But this conceptualization of feminism erased a vast array of heterosexual feminisms by declaring them an impossibility, an idea that, thankfully, has little traction now. Lesbian feminists of color, such as those involved in the Black feminist Combahee River Collective, pointed to the essential role of alliances with men of color to survive and resist racism, poverty, and systemic oppression. It was also undeniable that women around the world who were in relationships with men were also establishing life-saving feminist projects that attended to the daily needs of women and girls by acknowledging, without judgment, the actual conditions of their lives. And more, straight women were often on the front lines of the movement to raise *men's* consciousness about patriarchy, an absolutely vital part of the feminist project. We can now see that to abandon straight women, to erase their feminist contributions, to declare them a lost cause, and/or to pathologize their attraction men is not only embarrassingly sanctimonious but also an utterly ineffective strategy for creating gender justice.

10. Lorde, "Uses of the Erotic," 58.
11. Cheryl Clarke, "New Notes on Lesbianism" (1983), in *The Days of Good Looks: The Prose and Poetry of Cheryl Clarke, 1980 to 2005* (Boston: Da Capo, 2006), 81.
12. Radicalesbians, "Woman-Identified Woman," 172–177.
13. This is the logic behind the claim that "boys will be boys," a notion with broad political implications as demonstrated by thousands of white women Trump supporters, for instance, who chalked up Trump's boasting about sexual assault to normal behavior for men.
14. Indiana Seresin, "On Heteropessimism: Heterosexuality Is Nobody's Personal Problem," *New Inquiry*, October 9, 2019, https://thenewinquiry.com.
15. Adrienne Rich, "Compulsory Heterosexuality and Lesbian Existence," *Signs: Journal of Women in Culture and Society* 5, no. 4 (1986): 631–659.
16. Boys and men are typically socialized to have a more visual and aggressive relationship to sex than girls and women do; see, for instance, Beth Eck, "Men Are Much Harder: Gendered Viewing of Nude Images," *Gender & Society* 17, no. 5 (2003): 691–710.
17. Radicalesbians, "Woman-Identified Woman," 176.
18. Naomi Wolf, "Radical Heterosexuality," in *Women's Lives: Multicultural Perspectives*, ed. Gwyn Kirk and Margo Okazawa-Rey (New York: McGraw-Hill, 2004), 144.
19. Esther Perel, *Mating in Captivity: Unlocking Erotic Intelligence* (New York: Harper, 2007), 37.
20. Harry Hay, *Radically Gay: Gay Liberation in the Words of Its Founder*, ed. Will Roscoe (Boston: Beacon, 1997).

21. Joan Nestle, *The Persistent Desire: A Femme-Butch Reader* (New York: Alyson, 1992).
22. Audre Lorde, *Zami: A New Spelling of My Name* (London: Persephone, 1982).
23. Dorothy Allison, "Her Body, Mine, and His," in *Leatherfolk: Radical Sex, People, Politics and Practice* (Boston: Alyson Books, 1991), 46–47.
24. Jeanne Cordova, *When We Were Outlaws: A Memoir of Love and Revolution* (Tallahassee, FL: Spinsters Ink, 2011).
25. Cherríe Moraga, "The Slow Dance," in *Loving in the War Years* (Boston: South End, 1983), 26.
26. Tovia Smith, "This Chef Says He's Faced His #MeToo Offenses. Now He Wants a Second Chance," National Public Radio, October 7, 2019, www.npr.org; Lucia Graves, "How Famous Men Toppled by #MeToo Plot Their Comeback," *The Guardian*, May 27, 2018, www.theguardian.com.

SEXUAL CULTURES
General Editors: Ann Pellegrini, Tavia Nyong'o, and Joshua Chambers-Letson
Founding Editors: José Esteban Muñoz and Ann Pellegrini

Titles in the series include:

For a complete list of books in the series, see
www.nyupress.org

# Index

# About the Author

**Jane Ward** is Professor of Gender and Sexuality Studies at the University of California, Riverside, where she teaches courses in feminist, queer, and heterosexuality studies. She is the author of *Not Gay: Sex between Straight White Men* (NYU Press, 2015) and *Respectably Queer: Diversity Culture in LGBT Activist Organizations.*